PEOPLES
of
AFRICA

Burkina Faso

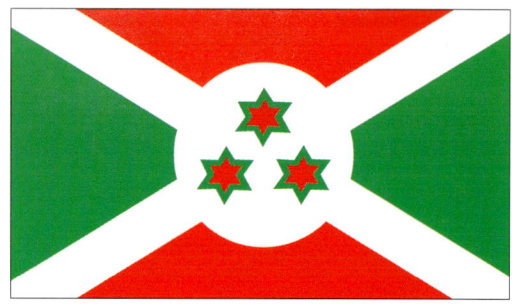
Burundi

Cameroon

Cape Verde

Central African Republic

Chad

Comoros

PEOPLES
of
AFRICA

Volume 2
Burkina Faso–Comoros

MARSHALL CAVENDISH
NEW YORK • LONDON • TORONTO • SYDNEY

Marshall Cavendish Corporation
99 White Plains Road
Tarrytown, New York 10591-9001

Reference Edition 2003

©2001 Marshall Cavendish Corporation

All rights reserved. No part of this book may be reproduced or utilized in any form or by any means, electronic or mechanical, including photocopying, recording, or by any information storage and retrieval system, without prior written permission from the publisher and the copyright holders.
Consultants:
Bryan Callahan, Department of History, Johns Hopkins University
Kevin Shillington

Pronunciation Consultant: Nancy Gratton

Contributing authors:
    Fiona Macdonald
    Elizabeth Paren
    Kevin Shillington
    Gillian Stacey
    Philip Steele

Discovery Books
    Managing Editor: Paul Humphrey
    Project Editor: Helen Dwyer
    Text Editor: Valerie J. Weber
    Design Concept: Ian Winton
    Designer: Barry Dwyer
    Cartographer: Stefan Chabluk

Marshall Cavendish
    Editorial Director: Paul Bernabeo
    Editor: Marian Armstrong

The publishers would like to thank the following for their permission to reproduce photographs:
    Corbis (Yann Arthus-Bertrand: 84); Mary Evans Picture Library (66); Hutchison Library (Robert Aberman: 53; Christina Dodwell: 74, 99, 103; Andrew Eames: 77; Sarah Errington: 67, 92, 96; Mary Jelliffe: 61, 87; Edward Parker: 68, 69; Stephen Pern: 59, 60); Christine Osborne/Middle East Pictures (89); Panos Pictures (Edgar Cleijne: 100; Howard Davies: 63; Jeremy Hartley: 57, 93; Fred Hoogevorst: 54; Giacomo Pirozzi: 65, 79, 80, 81, 85, 94, 95, 101, 102; Magnus Rosshagen: 82; Chris Sattlberger: 62); Edward Parker (73); Still Pictures (Edgar Cleijne: 90, 97; Mark Edwards: 50, 55, 56, 70, 71, 72, 75; Paul Harrison: 52; Margaret Wilson: 86)

(cover) Burkinabe women take lunch to their husbands in the fields during harvest.

Editor's note: Many systems of dating have been used by different cultures throughout history. *Peoples of Africa* uses B.C.E. (Before Common Era) and C.E. (Common Era) instead of B.C. (Before Christ) and A.D. (Anno Domini, "In the Year of the Lord") out of respect for the diversity of the world's peoples.

Library of Congress Cataloging-in-Publication Data

Peoples of Africa.
        p. cm.
    Includes bibliographical references and index.
    Contents: v. 1. Algeria–Botswana — v. 2. Burkina–Faso-Comoros — v. 3. Congo, Democratic Republic of–Eritrea — v. 4. Ethiopia–Guinea — v. 5. Guinea-Bissau–Libya — v. 6. Madagascar–Mayotte — v. 7. Morocco–Nigeria — v. 8. Réunion–Somalia — v. 9. South Africa–Tanzania — v. 10. Togo–Zimbabwe — v. 11. Index.
    ISBN 0-7614-7158-8 (set)
    1. Ethnology—Africa—Juvenile literature. 2. Africa—History—Juvenile literature. 3. Africa—Social life and customs—Juvenile literature. I. Marshall Cavendish Corporation.

GN645 .P33 2000
305.8'0096—dc21

99-088550

ISBN 0-7614-7158-8 (set)
ISBN 0-7614-7160-X (vol. 2)

Printed in Hong Kong

06   05   04   03   6   5   4   3   2

Contents

Burkina Faso — 50–57
    Land of the Mossi — 51
    The French Colonize — 52
    Independence and After — 53
    The Burkinabe Today — 54
    Life in the Countryside and in the Cities — 55

Burundi — 58–63
    The Land of the *Mwami* — 58
    Conflict Brings Chaos — 60
    Peoples, Languages, and Faiths — 61
    Farmers Crowd the Hillsides — 62
    Family Life — 63

Cameroon — 64–75
    Migrations of the Bantu-speakers — 65
    The Age of the Slave Trade — 66
    The Rise of Islam — 66
    Colonization and Independence — 67
    Cameroon Today — 68
    The People of Cameroon: Daily Life and Culture — 70
    The Bamileke: Farmers and Traders — 71
    The Fang: Farmers and Hunters of the South — 71
    Muslims and *Kirdi*: The Northern Peoples — 71
    Living in the Rain Forest — 73
    Masks, Art, and Music — 74

Canary Islands — 76–77
    Atlantic Crossroads — 76

Cape Verde — 78–81
    Surrounded by the Sea — 78
    Survivors — 80

Central African Republic — 82–87
    The Ancient Heartland — 83
    Under French Rule — 83
    Stolen Diamonds — 84
    Traders and Farmers — 84
    Everyday Life — 85
    Peoples of the Plateau — 86
    A Common Language — 87

Ceuta and Melilla — 88–89
    A Foothold in Africa — 88

Chad — 90–97
    Beyond the Desert — 91
    The French Colony — 92
    War and Drought — 93
    Hopes and Fears — 94
    Chad's Peoples: How They Live — 94

Comoros — 98–103
    The Islands of the Moon — 98
    A Troubled Modern State — 99
    Perfume and Poverty — 100
    The Comorian Way of Life — 102

Glossary — 104

Further Reading — 106

Index — 107

Peoples of Africa

BURKINA FASO

BURKINA FASO IS A LANDLOCKED COUNTRY IN WESTERN AFRICA. It lies on the southern fringes of the Sahara Desert.

In the north the land is dry and becomes part of the Sahara. Most of central Burkina Faso lies on a savanna plateau averaging 650 to 1,000 feet (200 to 300 meters) above sea level. The land here is typical of much of tropical Africa with scattered trees, bushes, and grassland. In the south the land is green with forest and fruit trees. The upper waters of the Red and White Volta Rivers flow through Burkina Faso, but they are too shallow for boats in the dry season.

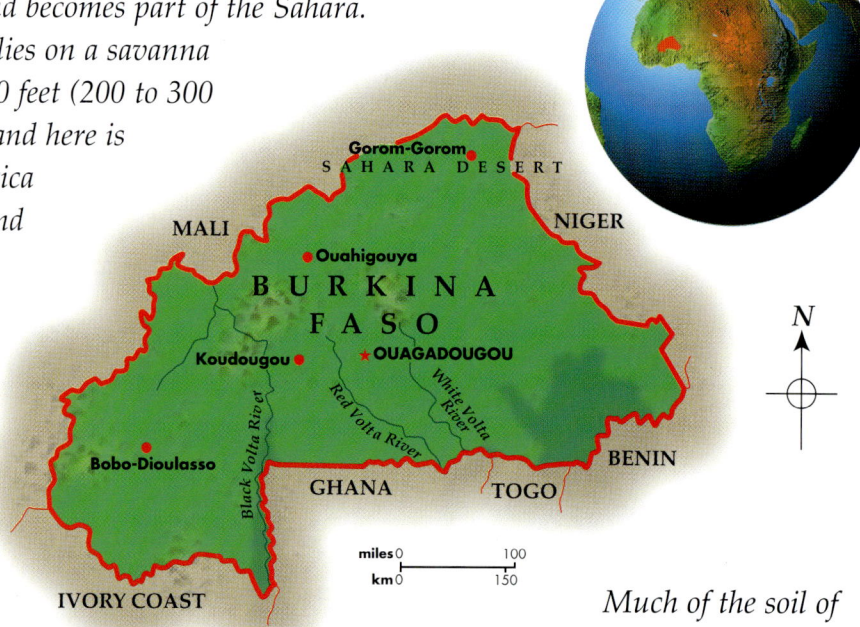

Much of the soil of Burkina Faso is poor, making it difficult for farmers to grow crops successfully. In recent years the climate has become much drier, and severe droughts have plagued the country, especially in the north.

CLIMATE

Burkina Faso has a hot, tropical climate. The dry season lasts from November to May and the rainy season from June to October. In the north, hot desert winds increase dryness.

Average January temperature: 76°F (24°C)
Average July temperature: 83°F (28°C)
Average annual precipitation:
  in north: 10–20 in. (25–50 cm)
  in south: 40–50 in. (100–127 cm)

Near Gorom-Gorom in the north, nomad girls pump water from a well. In recent years many new wells and boreholes have been dug to improve water supplies to rural areas.

BURKINA FASO

Land of the Mossi

There are no written records about the early history of the people of Burkina Faso (buhr-KEE-nuh FAH-soe), and the study of archaeology and languages provides little information. Iron and ceramic objects have been found that reveal the way people lived, but archaeologists have not been able to date exactly when these objects were made.

The first people in the region almost certainly lived by hunting animals, gathering wild fruits and vegetables, and catching fish in local rivers. After these people came the known ancestors of the present inhabitants of Burkina Faso. These peoples settled in the area between four and five thousand years ago. They became farmers, growing crops such as millet and sorghum. They later learned how to work with iron to make weapons and tools, which they used to clear the forest and plant more crops.

The Mossi (MOE-see) arrived in this area sometime between the eleventh and thirteenth centuries. They set up seven small but powerful kingdoms. These Mossi kingdoms are less famous in west African history than the great empires of Ghana, Mali, and Songhai for two main reasons. Since the Mossi kingdoms were not rich, they remained small at first. They had few natural resources, so the main trade routes from the forests of western Africa across the Sahara Desert did not pass through their lands. Second, western Africans south of the Sahara had no written languages in these times, and Muslim scholars from the north wrote much of the known history of western Africa. Since the Mossi people fought hard to defend their territory and resisted those who tried to convert them to Islam, no Muslim scholars lived within the Mossi kingdoms to record their early history.

For many centuries ordinary Mossi peasants were both farmers and warriors who learned to fight on foot and on horseback. These peasant-warriors gave the small kingdoms the strength to resist invasions from powerful empires such as Mali and Songhai. In turn, their cavalry

FACTS AND FIGURES

Status: Independent state

Capital: Ouagadougou

Major towns: Bobo-Dioulasso, Koudougou, Ouahigouya

Area: 105,869 square miles (274,200 square kilometers)

Population: 11,600,000

Population density: 110 per square mile (42 per square kilometer)

Peoples: More than 60 ethnic groups, including the Mossi (who make up just over half of the total population), Bobo, Grunshi, Lobi, Senufo, Busani, Samo, Dyula, Fulani, and Hausa

Official language: French

Currency: CFA franc

National days: Independence Day (August 5); National Day (December 11)

Country's name: Burkina Faso means "land of incorruptible men" in More, the Mossi language.

Time line:	First farmers settle in the area	Mossi peoples arrive	Era of the Mossi kingdoms
	ca. 3000–2000 B.C.E.	ca. 1000–1200 C.E.	ca. 1200s–late 1800s

Every morning as the sun rises, the King of the Mossi emerges from his palace in Ouagadougou to perform the centuries-old ceremony called "God rises."

raided weaker peoples and took slaves to sell in exchange for other trade goods.

The Mossi kingdoms saw themselves as members of the same family and rarely fought each other. If a Mossi kingdom was attacked by outsiders, other Mossi came to protect it. For nearly seven hundred years, the everyday life and the political systems of the Mossi evolved without interference from outside. Then, at the end of the nineteenth century, the French arrived.

The French Colonize

In the late nineteenth century, major European powers began to compete for control of Africa. The French seized a huge area of western Africa, including the Mossi kingdoms, which were finally conquered in 1896. The land and the peoples that today make up Burkina Faso became part of the federation of French West Africa, becoming a colony named Upper Volta.

The sixty years of French rule were often hard for the indigenous people. Much of the African land that the French had conquered was semidesert and had little economic value for the colonists compared to the British west African colonies. To raise money from their colonies, the French therefore introduced taxes (even children were taxed) and forced labor. People in Upper Volta were forced to grow cotton for the French to sell. Many families could no longer survive. As a result, nearly 100,000

French conquer the Mossi kingdoms	Region is a colony of France, called Upper Volta	Upper Volta becomes an independent state
1896	1896–1960	1960

Mossi people left their land and went to work on the cocoa plantations and in the gold mines of the British Gold Coast (now Ghana). Many men were recruited into the French army. The policy of forced labor split up families and caused much suffering and hardship.

Independence and After

After World War II both French and African political leaders hoped to create an independent federation of French West Africa, of which Upper Volta would be a member. Power would be shared equally in a French African community. However, in reality, the French were not prepared to treat Africans as equals, and richer countries such as Ivory Coast did not want to support poorer ones such as Upper Volta. In 1960 Upper Volta, along with other French colonies, became an independent state.

At first the government was a democratic one, until the first president, Maurice Yaméogo, banned all political parties. Strikes and demonstrations followed, and in 1966 the army seized power. Then, from 1970 to 1980, elected governments ruled until the army took control again in 1980. During the 1990s Burkina Faso gradually returned to democratic government, and in 1995 the Burkinabe (boor-kee-NAH-bae), as the people of Burkina Faso are called, took part in the first multiparty elections since independence. In the 1998 elections Blaise Compaore was re-elected president.

Thomas Sankara: The People's Leader

Captain Thomas Sankara was a young army officer who led a military coup in 1983. He wanted to use his power to free the Burkinabe from poverty. He changed the country's name from Upper Volta to Burkina Faso, or "land of incorruptible men," to give the people a sense of self-respect and dignity. Sankara encouraged the Burkinabe to build their own schools and health clinics, plant trees in deforested areas, and improve water supplies by digging new wells and building dams. To show that he was not above the ordinary people, Sankara rode a bike and made his government ministers give up their official luxury cars and drive smaller vehicles.

Sankara was impatient and changed things without proper planning. Opposition grew, especially among the wealthy. In 1987 he was assassinated, and a new military regime under Blaise Compaore took power. The new rulers promised to carry on Sankara's policies. Yet, in one of Africa's poorest countries, these rulers spent millions of dollars on a presidential palace. Today many Burkinabe regard Sankara as a hero.

1983–1987	1987	1990s
Captain Thomas Sankara in power; country renamed Burkina Faso	Sankara assassinated	Years of severe drought; country moves toward democratic government

The Burkinabe Today

The people of Burkina Faso speak several languages and belong to different ethnic groupings. They can be divided into two major west African language groups: the Voltaic and the Mande. Speakers of Voltaic languages make up nearly four-fifths of the population and include the Mossi, Bobo (boh-boh), Grunshi (GRUHN-shee), and Lobi (loh-bee). The Mande-speaking people, about one-fifth of the population, include the Senufo (seh-NOO-foh) (see IVORY COAST), Busani (boo-SAH-nee), Samo (sah-moh), and Dyula (JOO-lah). There are also some Fulani (foo-LAH-nee) and Hausa (HOW-sah) people (see NIGERIA). The Mossi are the largest and most powerful group; they account for more than half of Burkina Faso's nearly twelve million people.

The language of government is French, but in their everyday lives most people speak More, the Mossi language. Dyula is the main language used in trade.

Most Burkinabe follow their traditional African religions, but about 20 percent of the people are Muslim. A small number are Christian, and most Christians belong to the Roman Catholic faith, which the French brought to the region.

Although in recent times more people have chosen to follow Islam, many of these converts believe that the religion of their ancestors will teach and guide them. The king of the Mossi is a practicing Muslim, yet he still performs religious rituals according to the traditional beliefs of his ancestors.

Traditional religion teaches that spirits are everywhere in this world. They inhabit the trees and the fields, the rivers, and the uncultivated bush where wild animals are hunted. Each spirit has special powers that it can use to protect—or harm—individuals

> ## The Art of the Mossi
>
> *Storytelling, music and dance, sculpture, and jewelry making have all played an important part in the culture of the Burkinabe. Mossi artists are famed for their work in different art forms, including carved and painted wooden antelope masks, objects cast in bronze, and naturalistic wooden figures.*
>
> *Mossi kings were celebrated with bronze or gold statuettes made by the best artisan in the king's court. After creating the small statue, the artisan was not allowed to work again, so that the statuette was unique—and the most beautiful in the kingdom. Bronze statuettes are still made in craft workshops, but today they are sold in shops and street stalls.*

A woman from the Bobo people. Daily life for most Burkinabe women means hard work: collecting wood and water, pounding grain, cooking, and tending the crops.

and families. Spirits should be treated with honor and respect to ensure that they bring good rather than evil. Toward the end of the dry season people wear masks to honor the spirits of nature. The farmers hope that this will help to bring the rain so essential for healthy crops.

Ancestor worship is also important. Many Burkinabe believe that those who lived long ago, especially the kings and the chiefs, are still present in everyday life and should be respected.

The extended family remains at the center of many people's lives. Traditional leaders—especially the kings of the Mossi people—remain powerful. Stories of the great warrior-kings of the Mossi are handed down from generation to generation. The Mossi royal dynasty has existed for nine hundred years and is one of the oldest surviving dynasties in Africa. The king of the Mossi holds court in his palace in Ouagadougou (wah-gah-DOO-goo), where his followers come to seek advice on their problems. Even today the king can call upon thousands of warriors if he needs them.

Life in the Countryside and in the Cities

Most Burkinabe live in rural areas and farm small plots of land. Cotton is grown for home use and as the chief export crop. The main food crops are the tropical African

In local village markets such as this one, women earn a little extra money by selling surplus crops such as yams, bananas, and corn or by cooking snacks to sell.

Peoples of Africa

grains—millet, sorghum, corn, and rice—but families also grow some vegetables and fruits such as mangoes. Peanuts provide oil and are also a popular snack, often eaten raw or roasted with sugar.

Many farmers used to keep livestock, such as cattle, sheep, and goats, but today it is hard to find good grazing land. Years of low rainfall have dried up much of the land in the north, which is turning to desert, and the high population reduces the land available for farming in the south. Many Burkinabe have therefore left the countryside. Every year hundreds of thousands of young men travel south to find work in the cities and plantations of the richer countries of Ghana and Ivory Coast. Others move permanently to the towns and cities of Burkina Faso to find work there.

Burkina Faso is one of the poorest countries in the world, and industry and communications are underdeveloped. Most industry is based on the processing of raw materials, such as sugar, cotton, and edible oils.

Literacy rates in Burkina Faso are low. Less than one-third of children of elementary school age receive a basic education, although in recent years the government has made great efforts to improve educational opportunities.

Health facilities can be found primarily in populated areas. People living in towns have much better access to clinics and

Women taking lunch to their husbands in the fields during harvest. Lunch is often a thick porridge made from millet flour, served with a peppery sauce of vegetables or meat.

Africa's Film Festival

In recent years Burkina Faso has won an international reputation for cinema. Every two years it holds a Panafrican Film Festival known as FESPACO, the largest film festival in Africa. One of the best-known Burkinabe film directors is Idrissa Ouedreaogo. His film Yaaba, *meaning "grandmother," has won prizes at film festivals throughout the world.*

hospitals and to clean water. In rural areas people must often travel far to the nearest hospital, and they may not be able to afford the treatment. They often turn to local traditional doctors and to herbal remedies. More than half the country's women undergo the surgical procedure of female genital cutting (see SOMALIA). Life expectancy is low, and most Burkinabe cannot expect to live beyond their mid-forties.

Ouagadougou, the capital of Burkina Faso, is a bustling, windswept city full of small shops. The old and the new sit alongside each other. Donkey carts and motorbikes crowd the roads. Traditional leaders hold court before followers who bow to the ground in front of them. Yet at night, families watch television, and young people fill the cinemas and the discos to dance to reggae records and local bands.

A mosque and street stalls in Ouagadougou. The mosque is the heart of a Burkinabe Muslim's religious life. From the tallest minaret, Muslims are called to prayer five times a day.

Peoples of Africa

BURUNDI

BURUNDI IS A LAND OF STEEP GREEN HILLSIDES, RED EARTH, AND ROCKY PLATEAUS rising from the eastern shores of Lake Tanganyika.

Burundi's highlands rise from about 4,000 feet (1,200 meters) above sea level in the north to over 8,000 feet (2,400 meters) in the south. Burundi's soil was once rich, but heavy rains, pouring down on land stripped of its forest cover, have washed away much of the soil's fertility.

CLIMATE

Its high altitude keeps Burundi relatively cool. The two rainy seasons last from March to May and September to December.

Average January temperature: 73°F (23°C)
Average July temperature: 73°F (23°C)
Average annual precipitation: 33 in. (83 cm)

The Land of the *Mwami*

The first known inhabitants of Burundi (buh-ROON-dee) were the Twa (TWAH) people, who hunted animals and gathered roots, berries, and wild honey in the forests. The Twa were probably already living in the region in prehistoric times.

According to some historians, the Hutu (HOO-too) moved into Burundi about one thousand years ago and were followed some four hundred years later by the Tutsi (TOOT-see). The Hutu were farmers, part of the migration of Bantu-speaking peoples originally from western Africa (see CAMEROON). The cattle-herding Tutsi may have arrived from the Nile River region to the northeast. However, other historians now argue that ancestors of both the Hutu and Tutsi were already living side by side in Rwanda and Burundi many centuries before these dates.

During the 1500s C.E. in Rwanda, a social division developed between the two peoples (see RWANDA). The Tutsi became lords over the Hutu, protecting them in return for their work on the land. This

BURUNDI

FACTS AND FIGURES

Official name: *Republika y'Uburundi*

Status: *Independent state*

Capital: *Bujumbura*

Major towns: *Gitega, Bururi, Ngozi, Muyinga*

Area: *10,745 square miles (27,835 square kilometers)*

Population: *5,700,000*

Population density: *530 per square mile (205 per square kilometer)*

Peoples: *85 percent Hutu; 14 percent Tutsi; 1 percent Twa*

Official languages: *Kirundi and French*

Currency: *Burundi franc*

National day: *Independence Day (July 1)*

Country's name: *Burundi means "southern land" (as opposed to Rwanda, or "northern land") in the Kirundi language.*

and Tutsi alike. The Twa were considered to be on the bottom rung of traditional Burundi society. Both Hutu and Tutsi bartered crops and tools with them in exchange for game caught in the forests.

In the late 1800s, European explorers began to penetrate the kingdoms of eastern central Africa. Their chief concern was to bring these lands within the great European empires of the day and to exploit their natural resources.

In 1895 Ruanda-Urundi (Rwanda and Burundi) came under German rule. The Germans supported the existing pattern of rule in the region. However, they did not stay in power long. World War I broke out in 1914. Germany's enemies fought them in Africa as well as in Europe, and within two years Belgian troops had seized Ruanda-Urundi. After the war the League of Nations decided who would rule Germany's former colonies in Africa, and Belgium was the country chosen to govern Ruanda-Urundi.

system, very like the feudal system of medieval Europe, was called *buhake* (boo-HAH-kae). In Burundi a powerful kingdom developed in the late 1700s, with its capital located in the center of the country at Gitega. It was ruled by a Tutsi king, or *mwami* (oo-MWAH-mee).

In the mid–nineteenth century, power passed to local princes called *ganwa* (gahn-WAH). Their aristocratic status was thought to be more important than their Tutsi descent, and they ruled over Hutu

Tutsi herders tend their cattle. Traditionally, only the Tutsi people could own cattle. They considered farming the land to be dirty work, suitable only for the Hutu people.

Time line:	Twa living in Burundi region	The Hutu, a Bantu people, move into the region	Tutsi arrive	A kingdom develops around Gitega, with a Tutsi king	Ruanda-Urundi becomes part of German East Africa
	ca. 1000 B.C.E.	ca. 1000 C.E.	ca. 1400s	late 1700s	1895

When the Belgians moved in, they simply formed an extra rung, above the ganwa, in the existing hierarchy. These Europeans favored the Tutsi over the Hutu and gave them key jobs in the army and administration. The Tutsi now maintained their power as rich city dwellers and landowners rather than as feudal lords.

During the 1950s an independence movement emerged in Burundi. The eldest son of the reigning mwami, Prince Louis Rwagasore, led a political campaign based on unity between Hutu and Tutsi. Disliked by the Belgian authorities, he was assassinated with their backing.

Conflict Brings Chaos

Independence came in 1962, with Burundi separating from Rwanda, where a Hutu revolution had taken place from 1959 to 1962. The Hutu had overthrown the Tutsi, killing thousands (see RWANDA). To prevent something similar taking place in Burundi, Tutsi soldiers seized power and murdered thousands of Hutu peasants.

The strife became even more complicated in the 1970s. Some Hutu began a guerrilla war from the other side of the Tanzanian border and Tutsi troops killed innocent Hutu civilians in Burundi. The 1980s and 1990s saw political chaos, military coups, assassinations, civil war, and the murder of hundreds of thousands of people. Many thousands fled Burundi.

A brief period of hope glimmered from 1988 to 1993 under the leadership of Major General Pierre Buyoya, a Tutsi army officer.

> ## An Ethnic Conflict?
>
> *The conflict that has taken place in Burundi and Rwanda over the last forty years is often referred to as "tribal violence." This makes little sense. The Tutsi and Hutu are no longer organized along tribal lines, and there is even some doubt as to whether they can really be called separate ethnic groups. They both speak the same language, share the same religious beliefs, and live side by side. These days they follow much the same ways of life. In recent times, Tutsi have fought Tutsi and Hutu have fought Hutu. The conflict has more to do with power and politics and should be seen as a civil war rather than a tribal one.*

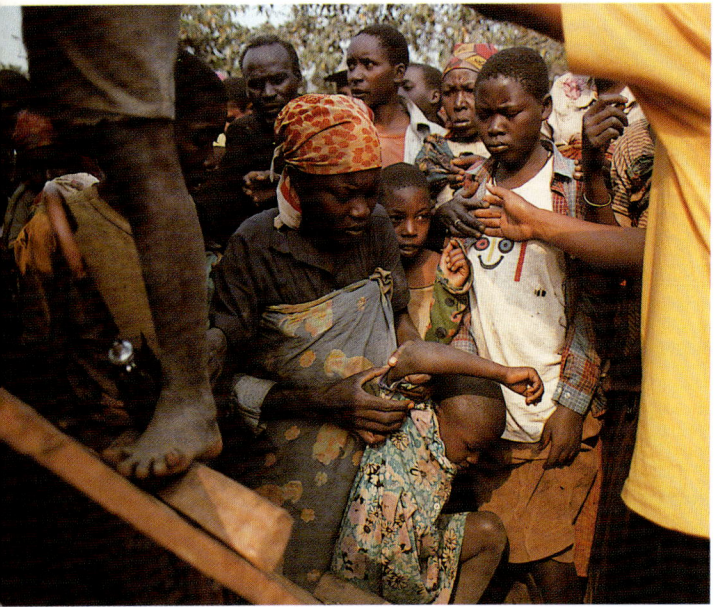

A mother gives her child a helping hand as anxious Hutu refugees climb aboard a United Nations truck. The violent conflict in Burundi has torn many families apart.

League of Nations authorizes rule of Ruanda-Urundi by Belgium	Burundi becomes an independent monarchy	Burundi becomes a republic	Hutu guerrillas attack. Tutsi reprisals kill up to 200,000 Hutu; 150,000 become refugees
1919	1962	1966	1972

The ground was prepared for nonethnic democratic politics, leading to the election in June 1993 of a moderate Hutu president, Melchior Ndadaye, who included both Hutu and Tutsi in his government. However, the Tutsi army would not accept a Hutu as president and assassinated him in October 1993.

In 1996 Buyoya seized power for the second time. His goal was to end the conflict, but he had no international backing. Burundi remains an area of potential strife, not because of its citizens, who struggle to grow their crops, improve their land, and rebuild their lives, but because of leaders who are more interested in power and the wealth it brings than in the well-being of their people.

Peoples, Languages, and Faiths

In Burundi the Hutu now make up about 85 percent of the population, while the Tutsi account for about 14 percent. The

The Sound of Thunder

Traditionally, the tall, slim Tutsi expressed themselves in spectacular leaping dances, wearing headdresses like lion manes. These impressive displays were used to express the prestige of the ruling class. Drums, too, played an important part in the life of the royal court. The drums were kept in a holy place, guarded by a priestess. They were made of hollowed logs and hide, and they were pounded with drumsticks. Fathers taught sons the rhythms of the drumming. A group called the Drummers of Burundi reached a worldwide audience for the first time in the 1980s. They influenced a range of popular Western musicians, from the founders of punk rock to Canadian folksinger Joni Mitchell.

Cloaked in scarlet, musicians carry large drums to a performance. Drumming is an important part of traditional culture in Burundi, as in many African countries.

Multiparty elections. Hutu president, Melchior Ndadaye, assassinated. Around 50,000 killed; 800,000 Hutu flee Burundi	Widespread civil war and massacres.	Pierre Buyoya, a Tutsi, seizes power; fails to end conflict
1993	**1994–1996**	**1996**

Twa form about one percent of the total. Most of their traditional forest homeland has been cleared for farming.

The common language of all three groups is Kirundi (kee-RUHN-dee), which belongs to the Bantu linguistic group. Swahili (swah-HEE-lee), the language of the eastern African coast, is used mostly for business and trade. French, spoken by the Belgian colonizers, is widely spoken and taught. The use of French tends to link Burundi culturally with central Africa rather than with the countries of eastern Africa, where the former colonial language is English.

About one-third of the population hold traditional religious beliefs. The Twa honor various spirits of the forests, while both Hutu and Tutsi believe the world was created by God, or Imana (EE-mah-nah), who can be reached through a figure called Kiranga (kee-RAHN-gah) or Ryangombe (ree-yahn-GOM-bae). Nearly two-thirds of the population are Roman Catholic, and there are small numbers of Protestant Christians and Muslims.

Farmers Crowd the Hillsides

Only 6 percent of Burundi's population lives in towns and cities; the countryside is densely populated. Most people are farmers, struggling to cultivate enough crops to feed themselves or to sell at the local market. They grow sweet potatoes, beans, peas, lentils, and bananas in the highlands and cassava along the river valleys and lakeshores. The chief export crop is coffee, along with small amounts of tea and cotton. Farmers raise cattle and pigs and export their hides. Large amounts of fish are caught in Lake Tanganyika or bred on fish farms.

Burundi has large reserves of peat around the Akanyaru River. It may also

The green Burundi countryside is dotted with fields, banana trees, and villages of round, thatched homes. Most of these are set within enclosed family compounds.

have as much as 5 percent of the world's nickel reserves, and oil has been discovered beneath Lake Tanganyika. However, selling those resources to the rest of the world remains difficult. First, the country is too far from seaports on the Indian Ocean coast to ship its exports easily to other countries. Second, the lack of surfaced roads and poor conditions during the rainy seasons make getting goods out of the country difficult. Finally, the long years of social unrest and civil war have devastated the economy, further increasing problems exporting goods.

These Tutsi children, pupils at a school in Bujumbura, provide hope for Burundi's future. Children must attend school until they are at least twelve years old.

Family Life

Poverty is widespread, and many people rely on foreign aid to survive. Over one-third of the population has no clean supply of drinking water, and disease is common. Life expectancy is only forty-eight for men and fifty-one for women.

Children must attend an elementary school from age seven to twelve, but teachers and resources remain in short supply. Many children have been orphaned or scattered during all the political unrest.

Women hold a low status in Burundi society. The man is the head of the household, and newly married couples live in the household of the husband's father. The family structure is traditionally an extended one, with many relatives remaining involved in family affairs and living within the same compound. Families belong to an *inuzu* (in-OO-zoo), or clan. Clan members share a common ancestor through the male line.

In Bujumbura, Burundi's capital, stand large buildings built in the European colonial style. Many government buildings in the capital are modern, built of brick, concrete, and sheet metal. Suburbs sprawl over steep mountain slopes. Traditional Hutu and Tutsi housing may be seen in the many hilltop villages in the countryside, surrounded by a patchwork of green fields. The homes often have brick or stone foundations, with a framework of timber forming the conical roof, which is thatched with straw. The traditional homes of the Twa were once of much the same shape, but they did not need to be so permanent or solid since the Twa hunters led a less settled existence, following game through the forests.

Peoples of Africa

CAMEROON

CAMEROON LIES BETWEEN WEST AND EQUATORIAL AFRICA. The Atlantic Ocean laps its southwestern coastline.

Cameroon's geography is extremely varied. In the south lies the coastal plain, which gives way to a region of dense rain forests. In the central region the land begins to rise, and the forests gradually give way to the savanna. At the heart of this region lies the Adamawa Plateau. In the far north the savanna gradually slopes down into marshland surrounding Lake Chad; here the Sahara Desert begins to encroach.

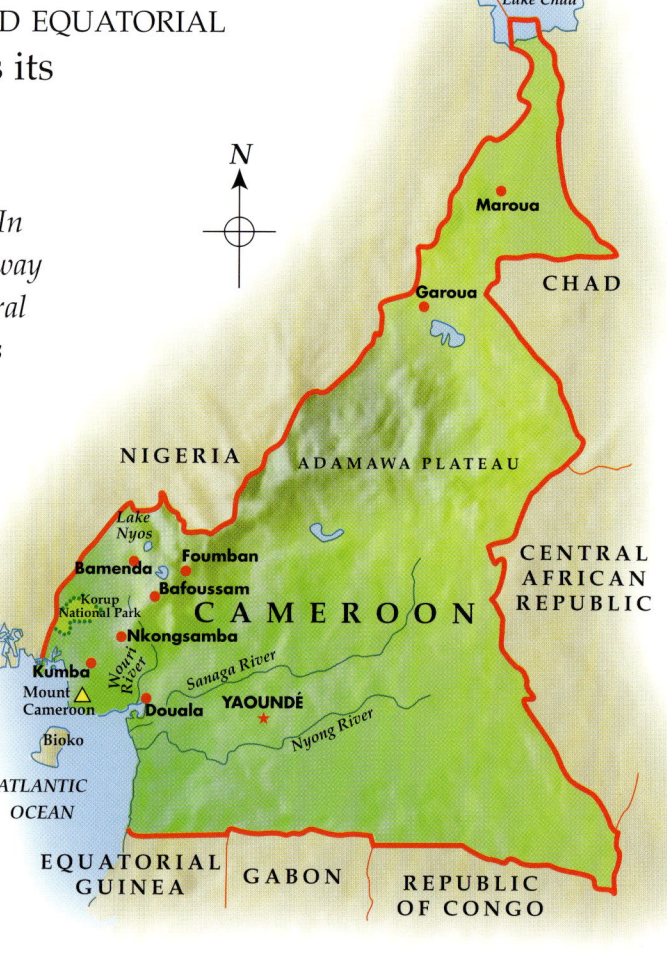

CLIMATE

Cameroon has a tropical climate. In the north the rainy season lasts from June to the beginning of October; the rest of the year is dry. In the south the rainy season is longer, between April and November. There is a huge difference in the amount of rainfall. Near Chad in the far north, there is hardly any rain; on the slopes of Mount Cameroon in the west, it rains nearly all the time—sometimes reaching 400 inches (over 1,000 centimeters) in a year.

	Yaoundé	Douala
Average January temperature:	76°F (24°C)	79°F (26°C)
Average July temperature:	73°F (23°C)	75°F (24°C)
Average annual precipitation:	62 in. (156 cm)	160 in. (403 cm)

High, forested mountains can be found in the west. Mount Cameroon, an active volcano that last erupted in 1982, is the highest peak at 13,350 feet (4,069 meters). Many streams and rivers wander through Cameroon. The volcanic soil in the west makes the land fertile, allowing for more crops and thus more people than in the dry north or the heavily forested south.

Migrations of the Bantu-speakers

No written records exist about the early history of the different peoples of the Cameroon (ka-muh-ROON) region. The earliest peoples were likely to have lived by hunting animals, gathering wild fruits and vegetables, and catching fish in local rivers.

Evidence from the study of archaeology and languages suggests that Cameroon (and part of eastern Nigeria) may have been the first homeland of the Bantu-speaking people. Today nearly 100,000,000 Bantu-speakers are spread throughout Africa south of the Sahara. Bantu, meaning "the people," is one of the major language groups of Africa; within this group are approximately seven hundred different, but related, languages.

The earliest Bantu-speakers in the Cameroon region may have included people who were forced to move southward as the Sahara dried up and turned to desert. By three thousand years ago, their farming, fishing, and hunting settlements had expanded to the south and east of Cameroon through the Congo equatorial basin. Around two thousand

> **FACTS AND FIGURES**
>
> **Official name:** Republic of Cameroon
>
> **Status:** Independent state
>
> **Capital:** Yaoundé
>
> **Major towns:** Douala, Garoua, Kumba, Maroua, Nkongsamba, Bamenda, Bafoussam
>
> **Area:** 183,569 square miles (475,442 square kilometers)
>
> **Population:** 15,500,000
>
> **Population density:** 84 per square mile (33 per square kilometer)
>
> **Peoples:** More than 150 ethnic groups, including Bamileke, Bamoun, Douala, Fang, Fulani, Gbaya, Hausa, Kapsigi, Margi, Mbum
>
> **Official languages:** French and English
>
> **Currency:** CFA franc
>
> **National day:** Independence Day (January 1); National Day (May 20)
>
> **Country's name:** The origin is not certain, but it probably comes from camerões, the Portuguese word for shrimps. The first Portuguese to reach the Wouri River in the fifteenth-century were amazed by the large number of giant shrimps they saw.

A young Baka boy hunts in the forest. There are only small numbers of hunter-gatherers in Cameroon today, but hunting skills have been handed down for thousands of years.

Time line:	Bantu-speaking farmers living in region	Ironworking technology spreads among Bantu-speaking peoples	Portuguese arrive on the Cameroon coast and begin trading
	ca. 1000 B.C.E.	ca. 1 C.E.	1480s

years ago, they learned ironworking technology, which greatly improved their farming and hunting capabilities and enabled them to spread across much of Africa south of the equator.

There is not enough evidence to explain why the Bantu began to migrate from the Cameroon region. However, some historians believe that it may have been due to a large increase in the population. This meant that there was no longer enough land available to grow crops to feed all the people.

The Age of the Slave Trade

Little is known of the history of the Cameroon region before the first Europeans reached the coast in the fifteenth century. There were no large states or famous kings, and most people lived in small communities. They passed down their history orally, through storytelling, music, and dance.

The Portuguese were the first Europeans to sail around the coast of western Africa in the fifteenth century. They began to trade with the coastal people, selling cheap iron, cloth, copper, and guns in exchange for goods such as ivory, gold, and pepper. They—and other Europeans such as the Dutch, British, and French—soon began to buy human beings as well. They wanted slaves to work on their new tobacco and sugar plantations in America and the West Indies. At first the Portuguese controlled the slave trade around the coast; later the Dutch, and then the British, took control. The slave trade was finally abolished in the nineteenth century. By then many millions of people from western Africa had been sold into slavery or had their families and communities destroyed.

An eighteenth-century print showing European trading ships off the Cameroon coast. The largest building was probably used to hold slaves until they were shipped to the Americas.

The Rise of Islam

In northern Cameroon, barely touched by the transatlantic slave trade, the history of the late eighteenth and nineteenth centuries is rather different. It was shaped by the arrival of the Fulani (foo-LAH-nee) people.

The Fulani are a nomadic people from the savanna regions of

Height of the transatlantic slave trade	Fulani establish Muslim states in northern Cameroon	Germany claims the colony of Kamerun	Kamerun divided between Great Britain and France after German defeat in World War I
1600s–mid 1800s	1800s	1884	1919

western Africa. Nomadic Fulani keep cattle and move from place to place in search of grazing land. Over the centuries numbers of Fulani have settled in different parts of the savanna of western Africa and have converted to Islam. They began to spread the word of Islam by peaceful methods and then by holy wars called jihads (ji-HAHDS). The Fulani played a major role in the history of western Africa.

Nomadic Fulani peoples began to gradually settle in northern Cameroon, establishing small Muslim states. They captured local non-Muslim peoples for slaves and drove them from the good grazing land to the rocky, infertile areas. The most powerful of these Muslim states was the Emirate of Adamawa, named after a famous Fulani leader, Modibo Adama.

Colonization and Independence

During the nineteenth century, slave traders were replaced by European missionaries and traders in other merchandise in the south. British traders began to dominate Cameroon's coastal economy. Soon the major powers in Europe began to compete for control of Africa. Germany claimed the Cameroon region as a colony in 1884, and it became known as Kamerun. In 1919, after Germany's defeat in World War I, a League of Nations' ruling divided Kamerun between Great Britain and France. Great Britain ruled the western zone and France the eastern zone, which made up almost 80 percent of the country.

After World War II, Cameroonians who wanted to be free from colonial rule set up their own political parties. Most wanted French and British Cameroon to be united as one and to be given back their independence. Full independence for French Cameroon was granted on January 1, 1960. The following year a

These Muslims of Foumban in western Cameroon are celebrating the end of Ramadan, the Muslim month of fasting, with a procession and dancing.

1960	1961	1972
French Cameroon granted independence	The north of British Cameroon opts to join Nigeria and the south to join French Cameroon in federation	Cameroon becomes united republic; new constitution

United Nations referendum allowed the people of British Cameroon to choose their future: the northern provinces chose to join Nigeria, the southern provinces to unite with the rest of Cameroon as a federal republic. In 1972 a new constitution was agreed upon, the federation was dropped, and Cameroon became a united republic.

Since independence, Cameroon has been largely peaceful. In a period of nearly forty years, there have been only two presidents: Alhaji Ahmadou Ahidjo, between 1960 and 1982, and Paul Biya since 1982. A coup was unsuccessfully attempted in 1984, after which the government clamped down on any opposition and ruled as a one-party state. During the 1990s the Cameroon government allowed different political parties, and opposition has grown stronger. There have been accusations of corruption and abuse of human rights among those who govern the country. Much of today's political conflict revolves around disputes between French- and British-oriented leaders.

A chief from the Balundu people. In rural areas, chiefs are still respected leaders of their local community; they administer the law and lead religious ceremonies.

Cameroon Today

The Republic of Cameroon has a huge variety of ethnic groups and languages. There are more than 150 ethnic groups, and the largest of these, the Bamileke, make up only about 15 percent of the population of Cameroon.

Twenty-four major African languages are spoken in Cameroon. In government and

Paul Biya becomes president	Unsuccessful attempt at coup; government rules as one-party state	Moves toward democratic government; opposition rises against corruption in government and abuse of human rights
1982	1984–1990	1990s

CAMEROON

Pidgin English

Pidgin English mixes English with one or more local languages and is often used for trade when people cannot understand each other's language. It is simpler than English, especially since grammar is often ignored. An English-speaking person hearing Cameroon Pidgin for the first time would recognize quite a number of the words, but would have difficulty following the speed and colorful way it is spoken. For example, in Pidgin I di tok *means "I'm talking."*

in high schools and universities, people primarily speak French and English. French is more widely used: four out of five people speak French and the rest speak English. When people trade with each other in the markets of Cameroon, they may speak French or English, but more often they speak some of the more common languages of western Africa so that traders from different parts of Cameroon or from neighboring countries such as Nigeria will understand. These languages include Hausa, Fulani, Douala, and Pidgin English.

Cameroon is above all a rural country where most people work as farmers. In the north many people live by keeping cattle. One of the few countries in Africa that grows enough to feed all its people, Cameroon does not need to import food. The main crops that people grow for their families include root vegetables, such as yams and cassava, cereals, such as millet, and different types of vegetables and fruits. Export crops include cocoa, coffee, and peanuts from the central region, cotton from the north, and palm oil from the forests of the south.

The discovery of oil off the coast made Cameroon a wealthy country in the 1970s and 1980s, and this, in turn, encouraged the development of other industries, including mining and logging. Unfortunately, because of government corruption, the majority of ordinary Cameroonians did not share in this wealth. During the 1990s the economy of Cameroon suffered as the world prices of oil, coffee, cocoa, and cotton all dropped.

It is estimated that about 40 percent of Cameroon's population is Christian and 20

An oil-palm plantation in southwestern Cameroon. The fruit of the palm is harvested and then used to produce a red-colored oil popular in cooking throughout western Africa.

percent is Muslim. Islam is practiced mainly in the north. The rest of the population follow different African religions. It is difficult to give accurate figures about religious beliefs because people often mix their religions. Many who are Christian or Muslim may continue to follow some of the religious practices of their ancestors.

The literacy rate in Cameroon is quite high for Africa; over 60 percent of the population can read and write. Over 40 percent of the population of Cameroon are under fourteen years old, and 75 percent of Cameroonian children attend elementary school. However, teachers are in short supply. The number of children attending school is lower in the north, where more children come from nomadic families and more traditional attitudes are common. Not all Muslim girls are allowed to go to Western-style schools; instead many Muslim children attend religious schools organized in keeping with the Koran, the holy book of Islam. There are several universities, including two in Yaoundé (yah-WUHN-dae).

Health facilities, including local clinics and hospitals, have expanded greatly since independence. Life expectancy in Cameroon averages fifty-seven years.

The People of Cameroon: Daily Life and Culture

In the rural areas most Cameroonians still live much as their parents and grandparents did. However, young people are moving to the towns and cities in large numbers in search of work and a more Western way of life. In doing so, some lose touch with the social traditions and values of the family and their ethnic group.

In contrast with rural people, urbanites live very different lives in cities such as Yaoundé, the capital, and Douala (doo-AH-lah), the main port. Here, most people live by trading, working in industry or in services, or by making things. They have more modern facilities, such as running water and electricity, if they can afford them. But in the cities there is unemployment, especially since the Cameroon economy declined in the 1990s, and this has led to a much higher crime rate.

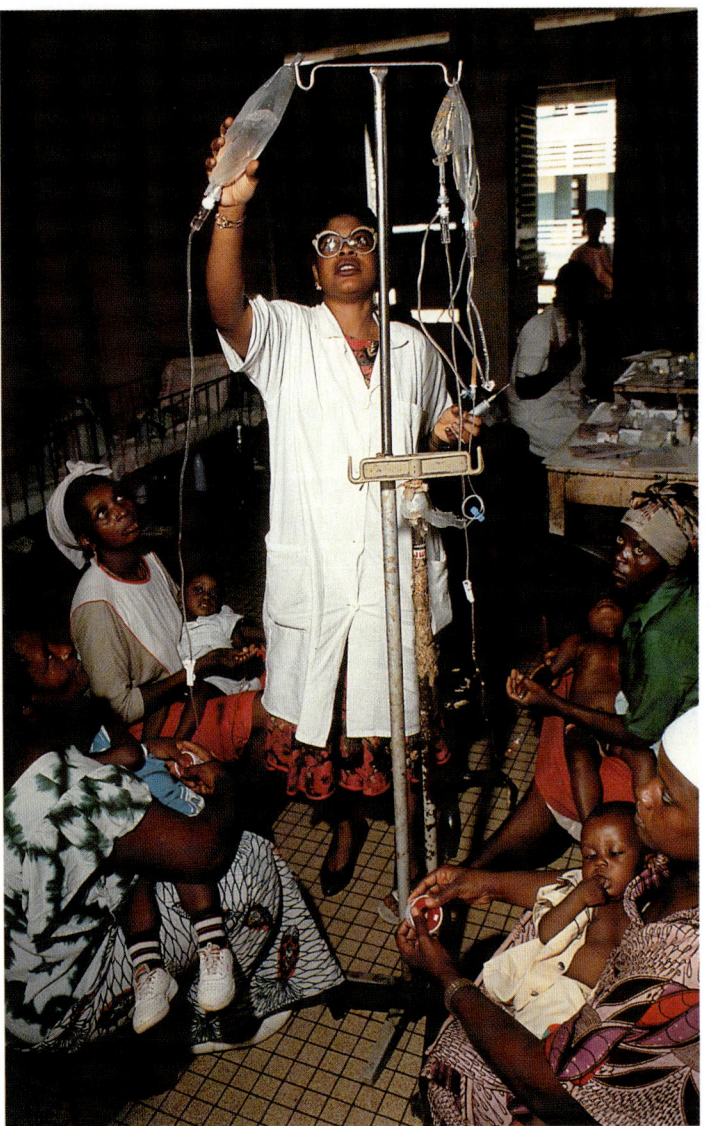

A doctor administers an intravenous drip to a sick child in the children's malaria ward in Laquintinie Hospital in Douala. Malaria is a serious disease in tropical Africa.

In the hills around Bamenda, a farmer tends his crop of medicinal plants. Farmers are now encouraged to grow these useful plants, which previously could only be found in the wild.

The Bamileke: Farmers and Traders

In western Cameroon, where the rich volcanic soil is excellent for farming, live the largest ethnic group, the Bamileke (bah-mee-LAE-kee). They live mostly in villages in distinctive houses with pyramid-shaped roofs.

Most Bamileke are farmers: the women grow the crops, while the men look after the cattle and work on the cocoa and coffee plantations. However, as the population in this area increases, more and more Bamileke are moving away to the towns and cities. Many have settled in Douala, the largest city and main port of Cameroon.

The Bamileke are divided into different independent chiefdoms. Their chiefs are responsible for holding on to the strong traditions of the Bamileke and are shown special respect.

The Fang: Farmers and Hunters of the South

In the forested parts of southern Cameroon live the Fang (FAHN-jee) people. They also make up part of the populations of Gabon and Equatorial Guinea (see GABON and EQUATORIAL GUINEA). The Fang live in small villages, growing mainly root crops and bananas and keeping domestic animals. They supplement their diet by hunting and fishing. In addition some farmers grow cocoa as an export crop. In recent times many of the young men have migrated to work in the timber industry, and the social values and traditions of the Fang have started to break down. Traditionally, Fang warriors were said to be the fiercest in Africa. Their bravery and conquests are kept alive through storytelling, poetry, and dance.

Muslims and *Kirdi*: The Northern Peoples

In the north of Cameroon are the Muslim Fulani and the small local ethnic groups called the Kirdi (KEER-dee). *Kirdi* is a Fulani word meaning "infidel," a person who follows a traditional religion rather

Peoples of Africa

Saving the Rain Forests

In recent years nearly half of the rain forests of Cameroon have been destroyed because trees have been cut down for timber by logging companies and land has been cleared for farming. A leading conservation organization, the Worldwide Fund for Nature, is working with the Cameroonian government to save the remaining forests. The rain forest of the Korup National Park in southwestern Cameroon has more species of plants than any other rain forest in Africa. Scientists have recently discovered a vine in Korup that has the potential to fight HIV infection.

Students paint a vibrant mural on their school wall to illustrate the beauty of the forest. Education can play a vital part in helping to save Cameroon's forests.

than Islam. The Kirdi include several smaller ethnic groups such as the Kapsigi (kup-SEE-gee) and the Margi (MAHR-gee). Both the Muslim Fulani and the Kirdi are rather cut off from the rest of Cameroon; development in the north of Cameroon is slower than in other parts, partly because the people of both groups want to hold on to their traditions and are resistant to change.

The Fulani people live in many western African countries (see GUINEA, MALI, NIGER, NIGERIA, and SENEGAL). In Cameroon, some Fulani are nomadic, moving from place to place with their cattle, while others have settled in towns and villages. Nomadic Fulani are usually Muslim, but they do not follow the religion strictly. Settled Fulani live mostly by farming and trade and are usually strict Muslims. Fulani men often marry more than one wife (the Muslim faith allows a man to marry four wives), and the different wives each live in separate houses.

Most Kirdi are poor, hardworking farmers. After they were driven into the rocky mountainous parts of northern Cameroon by the Fulani, they built distinctive round houses with tall roofs. The roofs themselves were unique because the side that faced a cliff was typically covered with grass. The Kirdi follow their own African religions, in which priests and others serve as intermediaries between the people and their ancestors and spirits.

Living in the Rain Forest

The original peoples of the African rain forests are small in stature, usually between 48 and 56 inches (1.22 to 1.42 meters) tall. Small numbers of these peoples, the Baka (BAH-kah) and the Kola (KOE-lah), live in scattered parts of the forests of southern Cameroon, mainly in small groups of about twenty people.

A forest village in southwestern Cameroon. Although modern materials are often used, these houses have traditional thatched roofs and fencing around the family compound.

> ## Lake Nyos: A Natural Disaster
>
> *In 1986 Lake Nyos, a small volcanic lake in the mountainous western region of Cameroon, made the world's headlines. In the middle of the night and without warning, the lake began to emit a poisonous mix of undetectable gases— carbon dioxide and hydrogen sulfide. In the morning dead cows, dogs, and other animals littered the lake's shore. Only a few people who lived in the villages around the lake woke up that day; nearly two thousand people died in their sleep. No one really knows what caused the lake to emit these gases but, according to experts, concentrations of these gases are rising again, and villagers have been moved out of the area.*

Nomadic hunter-gatherers, they normally do not stay in one place for very long. They make camps, building simple huts from branches and leaves, and hunt, fish, and gather wild plants for food and medicine. They have a deep understanding of the forest and all the plants and animals that live there. Since it brings them food, shelter, and medicine, the forest is at the heart of their religious beliefs. Although they have a unique way of life, these forest dwellers do not live in isolation. They meet and trade with farmers who live in nearby villages.

Masks, Art, and Music

Historically, art has played an important part in the lives of Cameroonians, although this is less true today, as more people move away from the villages to the towns. Strikingly beautiful, the art of the different peoples has been made for particular purposes and not merely for decoration or to please. For example, for the Mambila (mahm-BEE-lah) people, who live on the western border near Nigeria, art is important in the seasonal cycles of planting and harvesting and also for honoring ancestors. The Bamileke use masks in religious ceremonies. Worn during special celebrations, for example, to remember ancestors or at funerals, the masks keep the identity of the person secret and are supposed to give special powers.

Many Cameroonian artisans are highly skilled. Bamileke artisans are famous for their work, especially their carvings in wood, and are responsible for the richly decorated and carved buildings in the compounds where the chiefs and their wives

> ### Makosso: The Music of Cameroon
> *Probably the best-known pop music is* makosso *(mah-KOO-soo)—music unique to Cameroon. It is a blend of Cameroonian highlife (a form of African music that reflects European and American influences) and soul and makes great use of the electric guitar. The irresistible rhythms of makosso make people want to get up and dance. The most famous makosso musician is Manu Dibango (born 1933), a saxophonist, pianist, and composer who switched from classical music to jazz and in recent years has become an international pop star.*

A wood carving inlaid with beads by a Bamoun artist. Many Cameroonian peoples are famed for their elaborately decorated and dramatic wood carvings.

This dance in the highlands around Bamenda celebrates the people's relationship with the surrounding forest. The dancers wear masks, representing animals of the forest.

and children live. The Fang sculptors, said to be the best in Africa, are famous for their wooden figures, especially religious statues, and their drums and masks.

Music in Cameroon can be divided into that which is totally African and modern pop music, which shows the influence of America and Europe, such as in the use of the electric guitar. Traditional music is found more in the villages and pop music in the towns, although there is no rigid division, and modern musicians may often mix both styles. Traditional music and dance usually have a special purpose; different kinds of music and dance are performed for baptisms, weddings, and funerals, for chiefs, for women and men, and for hunters and warriors.

The Indomitable Lions

In Cameroon, soccer is an obsession. Not only have Cameroonian teams been successful on their own continent, winning the African Nations championship in 1984 and 1988, but the national team, called the Indomitable Lions, have taken part in four World Cups, reaching the quarter-finals in 1990 and thrilling football fans all over the world with their attacking play and strong running.

Peoples of Africa

CANARY ISLANDS

These volcanic islands lie about 70 miles (110 kilometers) west of Morocco, in the Atlantic Ocean. They are governed as two provinces of mainland Spain, which is 680 miles (1,100 kilometers) away.

The Canary Islands are strung out over 285 miles (460 kilometers) of ocean. The islands include green, irrigated valleys, dramatic mountains, pine woods, desert, and badlands of black volcanic lava.

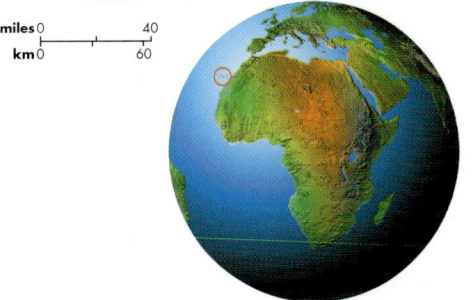

Atlantic Crossroads

The first known inhabitants of the Canary (kuh-NAR-ee) Islands were closely related to the Berber peoples who live in Morocco (see Morocco). They may have settled the islands about 2,100 years ago or even earlier. Now called Guanches (goo-AHN-chays), many were cave dwellers, although some built houses of stone and wood. They lived by herding sheep and goats, fishing, and growing barley. Guanche rock paintings and pottery have survived to this day.

In 1402 the Spanish kingdom of Castile conquered four of the islands. In 1479 Castile became part of Spain, which by 1496 ruled all of the Canaries. Most Guanches were enslaved and converted to Christianity.

CLIMATE

Lanzarote and Fuerteventura receive very little rain, resulting in desert or semidesert conditions. On the other islands the climate and vegetation varies according to altitude. The climate is warm, with mild trade winds. Eastern shores catch the harmattan, a dry winter wind that blows in from Africa's Sahara Desert.

Average January temperature: 64°F (18°C)
Average July temperature: 76°F (24°C)
Average annual precipitation: 8 in. (20 cm)

The Canaries became an important post for ships sailing between Spain and the Americas. In the 1500s irrigation was improved so that sugarcane could be grown, and the plantations first developed on Spain and Portugal's Atlantic islands were models for those in the Americas. On the Canaries, however, vineyards soon replaced sugar plantations.

During the 1800s many Canary islanders immigrated to Central and South America in search of a better life. In the twentieth century, long years of dictatorship by

General Francisco Franco, from 1939 to 1975, suppressed all calls for the islands' independence from Spain. After Franco died, terrorists demanding Canary Island independence began a bombing campaign. Today their organization has been absorbed into a democratic political party called the Canarian National Congress Party.

Industry dates back to 1927, when an oil refinery was built. Today's industries include chemical manufacturing and food and tobacco processing. Fishing communities thrive on most of the islands. Farmers grow bananas, potatoes, and tomatoes for export, and grapes are used in wine making. Irrigation is crucial. A large desalination factory near Las Palmas removes salt from seawater.

Apart from standard Spanish food, local cuisine includes many potato and fish dishes. Garlic, coriander, and red chilies go into hot, spicy sauces such as *salsa mojo* (SAHL-sah MOE-hoe).

Traditional island sports such as team wrestling and stick fighting are popular. Fiestas mark the holy days of the Roman Catholic Church. On January 5 the three kings of the Bible stories ride into town on camels. During the summer festival of Corpus Christi, beautiful designs made from flower petals decorate the streets.

Today's biggest moneymaker is tourism. But the loud music, clubs, and bars provided for tourists contrast sharply with the islands' traditional culture, which is devoutly Roman Catholic and conservative.

FACTS AND FIGURES

Official name: Islas Canarias

Status: Island provinces of mainland Spain

Provincial capitals: Santa Cruz de Tenerife, Las Palmas de Gran Canaria

Area: 2,810 square miles (7,278 square kilometers)

Population: 1,500,000

Population density: 534 per square mile (206 per square kilometer)

Peoples: Of mixed Guanche, Spanish, and other European descent; also European expatriate communities

Official language: Spanish

Currency: Spanish peseta

National and regional days: Canary Islands Day (May 30); Spanish National Day (October 12)

Country's name: The word canary comes from the Latin word canis, meaning "dog." The islands were possibly named by Roman seafarers after dogs they found living there.

Over the centuries the people of Lanzarote have become skilled at farming in a dry climate. The black volcanic soil produces grains, fruits, and vegetables.

Time line:	Possible date for Berber settlement	Spain conquers the Canaries	Plantations developed	Many islanders leave for the Americas	Terrorist campaign for independence	Spain joins European Community (today's European Union)
	ca. 150 B.C.E.	1400s C.E.	1500s	1800s	1970s	1986

CAPE VERDE

CAPE VERDE CONSISTS OF FIFTEEN ISLANDS lying about 370 miles (600 kilometers) off the coast of western Africa. Nine of the islands are inhabited. The nearest mainland countries are Mauritania, Senegal, The Gambia, and Guinea-Bissau.

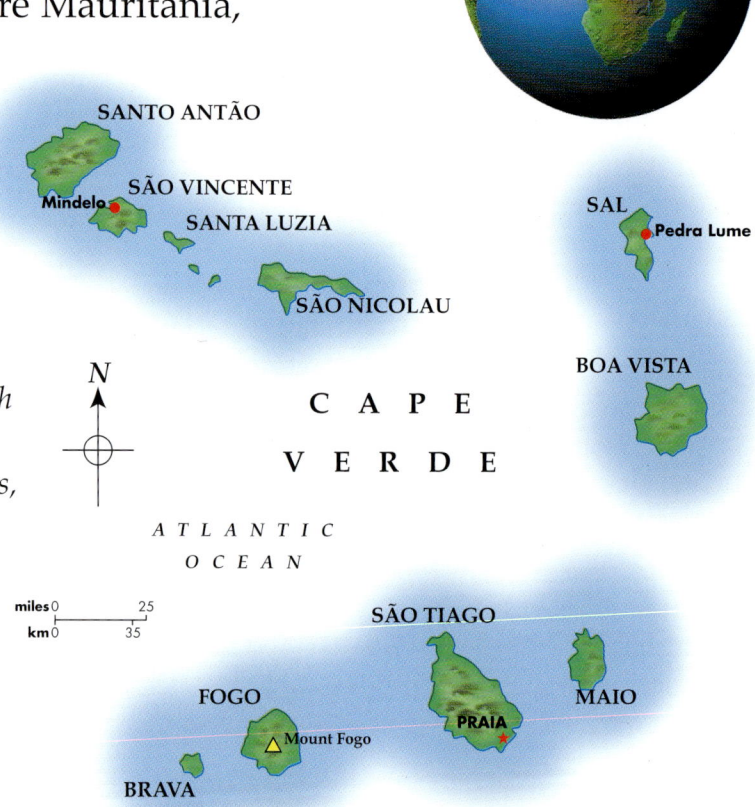

The Cape Verde Islands originated as volcanoes. The largest, Mount Fogo, towers 9,281 feet (2,829 meters) above sea level and is still active. Acacia trees grow on the steep mountain slopes, along with breadfruit, coffee, coconuts, and date palms. Corn, beans, sugarcane, bananas, and watermelons flourish in sheltered mountain valleys. The three easternmost islands are low, sandy, and windswept. People living there extract salt from seawater and catch tuna, shark, and flying fish.

Surrounded by the Sea

The Cape Verde (KAEP VUHR-dee) Islands are surrounded by the deep waters of the Atlantic Ocean. Strong currents running south along the Senegal coast kept the islands uninhabited for thousands of years. Portuguese sailors spotted the islands in 1456 C.E., and the Portuguese settled them shortly afterward. They established sugar plantations and brought slaves from the west African mainland to work on their plantations. From around 1500 to 1800, settlers also took part in the slave trade to the Americas. Slavery was finally abolished in Portuguese colonies in the mid–nineteenth century.

CLIMATE

Some years it hardly rains on Cape Verde. On the southern islands, though, dramatic thunderstorms and flash floods wash precious soil into the sea. From December to February, a warm, dry wind called the harmattan blows in from the Sahara Desert, filling the air with choking clouds of dust.

Average January temperature: 81°F (27°C)
Average July temperature: 86°F (30°C)
Average annual precipitation: 10 in. (25 cm)

From around 1800 onward, whaling ships from the United States voyaged regularly to Cape Verde, and the sea captains recruited sailors from Cape Verde as crew. Some of these sailors settled in American seaports, and people of Cape Verdean descent still live along the east coast of the United States. Cape Verde also became an important refueling station for steamships. Cargo boats and passenger liners stopped in the islands to load stocks of coal and fresh food on board.

Life on the islands was never easy. Water was always in short supply, and in 1747 a series of devastating droughts began. Thousands of people died from hunger and thirst; in the twentieth century many immigrated to western Africa, Portugal, and the United States.

FACTS AND FIGURES

Official name: *Ilhas do Cabo Verde*

Status: *Independent state*

Capital: *Praia*

Other town: *Mindelo*

Area: *1,557 square miles (4,033 square kilometers)*

Population: *450,000*

Population density: *289 per square mile (112 per square kilometer)*

Peoples: *71 percent mixed African-European (creoles or mestiços); 28 percent African; 1 percent European*

Official language: *Portuguese*

Currency: *Cape Verdean escudo*

National days: *National Heroes' Day (January 20); Youth Day (June 1); Independence Day (July 5)*

Country's name: *The name Cape Verde probably comes from the nearest location on the mainland, the Cap Vert Peninsula in Senegal. Cap Vert means "green point of land."*

Many colorful houses in colonial style still survive from the days when Portugal ruled Cape Verde. This house is in Mindelo, Cape Verde's most important port.

Until 1975 Portugal ruled Cape Verde. In 1956 educated Cape Verdeans began to campaign for independence, along with people in the African mainland colony of Portuguese Guinea (see GUINEA-BISSAU). After many years of fighting on the mainland, both countries won independence, and Cape Verde became a republic in 1975. Today it is a democratic, multiparty state. Everyone over the age of eighteen has the right to vote.

Time line:	Portuguese sailors land on uninhabited Cape Verde islands	Portuguese bring slaves from western Africa	Drought and starvation lead to mass immigration	Cape Verde becomes independent	New democratic, multiparty constitution takes effect
	ca. 1456 C.E.	1470s–1700s	1910–1950s	1975	1992

Peoples of Africa

Because the Cape Verde Islands get so little rain, drinking water is always in short supply. These children are waiting in line to fill metal or plastic containers with water.

Survivors

Cape Verdeans are proud of their successful survival in such a difficult environment and also of their multicultural society.

Most people on Cape Verde are of mixed African-European ancestry; nearly all the rest originate from western Africa. After the abolition of slavery, the few estate owners and slave traders returned to Portugal. Portuguese is the official language, but many people prefer to speak Crioulu, Cape Verde's own mixture of Portuguese and languages of western Africa. Almost all Cape Verdeans are Christian; about 75 percent are Roman Catholic. Several different Protestant groups and followers of traditional African beliefs add to the religious mix.

Many families have links with friends and relatives overseas. Households are often headed by women; they stay on Cape Verde to care for their children while their husbands work overseas and send money back home to support them.

Making Music

Cape Verde music combines Portuguese and African traditions. **Coladeira** *(koh-lah-dae-EE-rah) are fast, energetic dances based on African rhythms.* **Morna** *(MOOR-nah) are sad songs of loss, longing, and homesickness, which probably originated as slave laments. In the past, single-stringed African instruments were popular; the* **cimboa** *(sim-BOE-ah) was played with a bow, and the* **berimbau** *(ber-RIM-bow) was plucked with the fingers. Today they have been replaced by imported Portuguese instruments, particularly guitars.*

The most famous Cape Verdean singer is Cesaria Evora. With a strong, sweet voice, Evora sings the haunting morna laments with great feeling. Her 1995 album **Cesaria** *was released in more than twenty countries and nominated for a Grammy Award.*

Almost 70 percent of the people live in the countryside, farming small plots of land. In villages by the sea, the men earn money from fishing, while the women tend small vegetable plots. There is little flat land for building, so houses in towns and villages are often crowded together in narrow streets and squares. Many buildings show traces of Portuguese style, with whitewashed walls, tiled roofs, and pots of flowers in the windows.

Cape Verde is a youthful country; at least half the population is under sixteen. Education is free and compulsory for children aged seven to fourteen.

Government programs have almost wiped out malaria, which used to be a serious health problem. The average life expectancy is around sixty-four years for both men and women.

Cape Verde relies on money sent home by citizens working overseas and on aid from richer countries to survive. Since 1991 the government has made plans to encourage economic development, hoping to earn money from fisheries, tourism, and commercial services such as banking.

The islanders need to import about 90 percent of their food. To make themselves more self-sufficient, the Cape Verdeans have established many programs to save water, improve the environment, and enable more crops to be grown.

Staple foods include potatoes, plantains (a type of banana), cassavas, and yams. The national dish is *cachupa* (kah-CHOO-pah), a mixture of beans and corn or rice. Fresh-caught seafood, especially lobster, shrimp, and tuna, is made into spicy soup or cooked in dishes like "pastry with the devil inside" (tuna, tomatoes, and onions wrapped in a flour-and-potato mixture and deep-fried). Tropical fruits include mangoes, guavas, melons, and papayas. In the countryside people snack on raw sugarcane, while in the towns sticky fudge is made from locally produced sugar.

> ## Shrimp Soup
>
> *You will need:*
>
> *2 small green bananas*
> *1 teaspoon salt*
> *2 cups water*
> *2 onions*
> *4 tomatoes*
> *3 big potatoes*
> *1–2 cloves garlic, minced*
> *2 small chili peppers*
> *1–2 cups cooked, shelled shrimp*
> *2 cups boiled rice*
>
> *Peel and slice bananas and soak in saltwater for fifteen minutes, then drain. Wash and chop onions, tomatoes, and potatoes. Fry onions and minced garlic in a big pan until onions are clear, then add bananas, tomatoes, potatoes, chili peppers, and shrimp and cover with fresh water. Simmer until vegetables are soft and add boiled rice. Serve warm.*

These women are selling bread at an open-air market. Cape Verde cannot grow enough food to feed all its people, so wheat for breadmaking is imported from the United States.

Peoples of Africa

CENTRAL AFRICAN REPUBLIC

THE CENTRAL AFRICAN REPUBLIC LIES AT THE VERY HEART OF THE AFRICAN CONTINENT, just north of the equator.

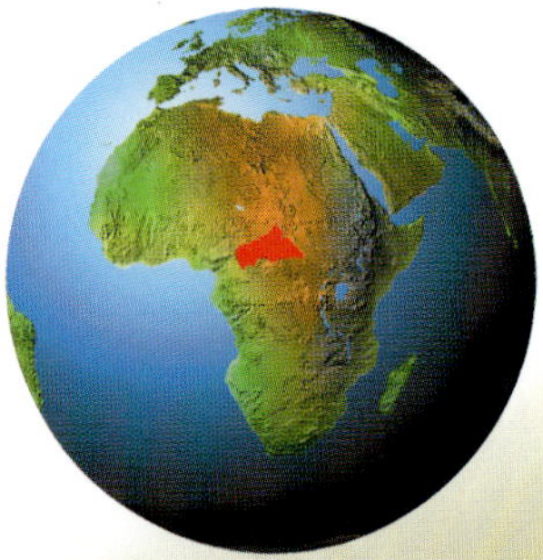

The Central African Republic occupies a large plateau that is about 2,000 feet (600 meters) above sea level. Grasslands cover most of the country. The northeast is dry and dusty, but in the southwest dense rain forests grow. Northern rivers flow northward towards Lake Chad. The southern part of the country lies within the Ubangi River basin, a tributary of the Congo River.

CLIMATE

The Central African Republic has an equatorial climate moderated by its height above sea level. The rainy season lasts from June to September in the north but is longer and heavier in the south.

Average January temperature: 80°F (27°C)
Average July temperature: 77°F (25°C)
Average annual precipitation: 61 in. (155 cm)

Women use a dugout canoe, or pirogue, to travel to market at Bangassou, on the Bomu River. This southern town lies on the border with the Democratic Republic of Congo.

CENTRAL AFRICAN REPUBLIC

The Ancient Heartland

Little is known about the early history of the region that today forms the Central African Republic, but archaeological evidence points to ancient settlement of the area. Megaliths (large standing stones) at Bouar (BWAHR), in the far west, were probably erected over 2,500 years ago.

The eastern part of the country lay on the borders of Sudan's Meroë (MEH-roe-wae) Empire (ca. 750 B.C.E.–350 C.E.; see SUDAN). By the 1500s C.E. two states governed the region: the kingdom of Gaoga (gah-OH-ga) ruled the north, while that of Anzica (AHN-zi-kah) ruled the south. The states lived by trading the fine craft work of the region, such as tools, spears, and carvings, and raiding neighboring territories for slaves.

Soon, however, they themselves were under attack from European and Arab slave raiders. Countless thousands were marched off in chains to the Atlantic ports to be shipped overseas or to the slave markets of Egypt. By the 1850s large areas of land had been depopulated. Azande, Banda, and Baya peoples moved in to occupy these areas.

Under French Rule

The Berlin Conference of 1884 to 1885, which decided how the European powers would seize African lands as colonies, set the region aside for the French. In 1899, France licensed seventeen private companies to exploit the region's rubber, timber, cotton, and mineral resources.

> **FACTS AND FIGURES**
>
> **Official name:** République Centrafricaine
>
> **Status:** Independent state
>
> **Capital:** Bangui
>
> **Major towns:** Berbérati, Bouar, Bossangoa
>
> **Area:** 241,240 square miles (624,812 square kilometers)
>
> **Population:** 3,400,000
>
> **Population density:** 14 per square mile (5 per square kilometer)
>
> **Peoples:** 34 percent Baya; 27 percent Banda; 21 percent Mandja; 10 percent Sara; the remaining 8 percent comprise smaller ethnic groups, including Babinga (or Aka), Zande, Yakoma, Banziri, and Burak
>
> **Official language:** French
>
> **Currency:** CFA franc
>
> **National days:** Boganda Remembrance Day (March 29); Independence Day (August 13)
>
> **Country's name:** The country's name is a description of its geographical location.

Many of the people were forced into labor and treated little better than slaves.

The territory was named Ubangi-Shari (oo-BON-gee SHA-ree) in 1894 and sixteen years later was joined with Chad, Middle Congo, and Gabon to form an official colony, French Equatorial Africa. These were unhappy years, with famine and constant rebellions. French troops fought a brutal war against the Baya people between 1928 and 1931.

During World War II (1939–1945), the country became a base for the Free French,

Time line:	Megaliths erected at Bouar	Kingdom of Gaoga rules north; kingdom of Anzica rules south	Arab and European slave traders devastate region	French create territory of Ubangi-Shari	Ubangi-Shari becomes part of French Equatorial Africa.
	ca. 500 B.C.E.	1500s	1600s–1800s	1894	1910

exiled forces who fought with the Allies against the Germans who were then occupying France. After the war, calls for independence arose, and Barthélemy Boganda founded the Movement for the Social Evolution of Black Africa. When independence came in 1960, David Dacko, a pro-French candidate, became president.

Stolen Diamonds

In 1966, amid mounting economic problems, Colonel Jean-Bédel Bokassa seized power. A thirteen-year reign of terror based on murder and corruption followed. During this period Bokassa misappropriated a personal fortune, much of it in diamonds. In 1979 he ordered the murder of over one hundred teenage protesters, and world opinion demanded that he be forced to resign from power. French troops reinstated David Dacko, who was still a loyal ally of France.

Trouble in the Central African Republic was not over. Dacko was overthrown again in 1981, and André Kolingba became president. He made the Central African Republic a one-party state, and protests against injustice increased once again. In 1993 Ange-Félix Patassé became president in a multiparty general election. Patassé came from the central region of the country, and for the first time political power no longer belonged to the southern elite who had held power since independence.

In 1996, amid growing economic problems, the army rebelled against the government because army members were not being paid. Again the French army was brought in to restore order. Today, after a peace agreement between the two sides, Patassé remains in power. Although the Central African Republic is far from stable, the terrible years of the Bokassa regime are now far behind, and people can look forward to the future. However, the immediate problems of national debt and widespread poverty are immense.

In 1977 Jean-Bédel Bokassa crowned himself ruler of the Central African "Empire." He spent $20 million on the coronation. Just two years later, he was overthrown.

Traders and Farmers

The Central African Republic is landlocked at the center of the continent. The roads are poor, particularly in the rainy season,

Country gains independence. David Dacko elected first president	Coup by Jean-Bédel Bokassa	Dacko regains power with French help	André Kolingba overthrows Dacko	Ange-Félix Patassé wins multiparty presidential elections	Army mutinies; French soldiers brought in to restore order
1960	1966	1979	1981	1993	1996

Women attend a literacy class, copying words onto slates. Only 25 percent of women in the Central African Republic can read and write, compared with 52 percent of men.

making water transportation crucial, whether by canoe or riverboat. Exports are transported by river from Bangui (bon-GEE) down to Brazzaville in the Republic of Congo, and from there by rail to Pointe-Noire, also in the Republic of Congo, a total distance of 1,050 miles (1,690 kilometers).

The Central African Republic contains large, unexploited reserves of uranium at Bakouma in the south, as well as diamonds, gold, and silver. Cotton is a valuable crop. Less important cash crops include coffee, peanuts, rubber, and tobacco. The rain forests produce hardwoods such as mahogany and obeche, which are exported.

Many people farm small plots of land, producing just enough food to feed their families and supply the local market. Grain crops in the north include millet and sorghum. In the west, farmers grow plantains (cooking bananas), yams, okra, and corn. Cotton and cassava grow in the humid south. The rivers provide fish.

Everyday Life

The long years of political and economic troubles have created difficult social conditions in the Central African Republic. Elementary education is supposed to be compulsory for children between the ages of six and fourteen, but many miss out on schooling altogether. Doctors struggle to cope with malaria and malnutrition, and AIDS is a major problem, especially in Bangui. Life expectancy is only forty-eight for men and fifty-three for women.

During the French colonial period, education and health care were largely in the hands of Christian missionaries. Today over a third of the population is Roman Catholic or Protestant. There are a number of Muslims, too. Well over half of the people follow traditional African beliefs in spirits, witchcraft, and healing, beliefs often expressed in ritual dances.

Traditionally, the peoples of the Central African Republic lived in the country, many of them scattered across remote areas of scrubland. French colonial policy forced them to move into areas where they could provide a workforce for the plantations. Under Bokassa many were forced to move to areas served by the network of roads. Today almost half of the population lives in or around the towns.

The center of the capital, Bangui, is built in the French colonial style. Outer suburbs sprawl along the roadsides, with busy street markets and stops for trucks and minibuses, which provide the most common forms of transportation and are loaded to the brim with passengers. Conditions in the towns are makeshift and often unhealthy. Most town dwellers have to drink water from street faucets. This water is often contaminated with sewage and causes diseases such as cholera.

In country villages, timber, mud, corrugated iron, and straw matting provide building materials. The traditional home design is round, with walls of dried mud topped with a conical, thatched roof. Most men wear Western-style clothes, but women wear brightly patterned cotton wraps and turbans.

Peoples of the Plateau

The Central African Republic is a land of many different peoples. The longest established are probably the Babinga (bah-BING-gah), or Aka (AH-ka), about fifteen thousand of whom live in the southwestern rain forest around Mbaïki (um-BAE-kee). They live by hunting and gathering forest foods. The Babinga are descended from the short, slightly-built peoples who were the original inhabitants of the equatorial forests and are closely related to the Aka and Baka people in the Republic of Congo and Cameroon (see CONGO, REPUBLIC OF, and CAMEROON).

The country's three largest ethnic groups, the Banda (BAHN-dah), Baya (BAH-yah), and Mandja (MAHN-jah), live in the western part of the country. Together they make up over 80 percent of the population. They are mostly farmers and traders.

The Sara (SAHR) live in the grain-growing lands of the north as well as across the border in Chad (see CHAD). The Zande (ZAHN-dee) live in the eastern regions adjoining the Democratic Republic of Congo and southern Sudan.

The Banziri (bahn-ZEE-ree) and Yakoma (yah-KOE-mah) in the south are peoples of the great rivers, skilled with boats and fishing. These peoples make pirogues, or

Dressed in banana leaves, this Babinga man was elected by the people in his village to perform a good luck dance before an elephant hunt.

CENTRAL AFRICAN REPUBLIC

Food and Drink

- **Chicken or pork:** *Many country families keep pigs and chickens but eat meat sparingly.*

- **Fish:** *The Ubangi River serves as an important source of fish. Fish are preserved by smoking over a fire or drying in the sun.*

- **Cassava:** *This root crop must be soaked in water and then dried in the sun. When it is ready, it is pounded into a starchy flour, which is mixed with water and made into a type of stiff porridge. It is served with a vegetable sauce, or gombo (GOM-boe), that might include tomatoes, chilies, or okra.*

- **Alcoholic drinks:** *A strong, cloudy beer is made from millet. Palm wine is another strong alcoholic drink, made from the sap of a type of palm.*

- **Tropical fruits:** *Mangoes, bananas, and papayas flourish in the equatorial climate.*

A Common Language

Each of the ethnic groups in the Central African Republic has its own language or dialect. The former colonial language, French, remains in official and widespread use. Many traders use Arabic in the north of the country, Hausa (HOW-sah) (the most widespread of the west African languages) in the west, and Swahili (swah-HEE-lee) (the language of the East African coast) in the east. However, the Central African Republic also has a national language called Sango (SAHN-goe), originally spoken by the river traders of the south. It gradually borrowed words from other languages, including French. Although Sango is spoken as a first language by only 7 percent of the population, it is now commonly used throughout the country to allow people who speak different languages to communicate with each other.

A Sango-speaking family from the south of the country outside their home. Their dwelling is typical of the region, brick-built with a roof of overhanging thatch.

canoes, from hollowed-out hardwood tree trunks. The Banziri and Yakoma were the first to come in contact with the French in the 1880s. They were educated by the French, and many found jobs in the colonial administration. Their privileged positions led to their domination of the government, trade, and culture of the independent Central African Republic up until the 1990s.

Peoples of Africa

CEUTA AND MELILLA

TWO TINY POCKETS OF SPANISH TERRITORY, Ceuta and Melilla, lie on the coast of Morocco.

The port of Ceuta is built on the southern shores of the Strait of Gibraltar. Melilla is located about 135 miles (215 kilometers) to the east on the eastern side of a rocky peninsula, Cape Tres Forcas.

A Foothold in Africa

The first known settlers of Ceuta (THAE-oo-tah) and Melilla (muh-LEE-lyah) were Phoenicians from Carthage (in present-day Tunisia). Both ports had become part of the Roman Empire by 44 C.E. By 711, Arab armies had brought Islam to all of northern Africa and to the Berber peoples of the region. The north Moroccan coast became a center of Islamic learning and scholarship.

Ceuta was seized by Portugal in 1415. In 1497, Spain captured and fortified Melilla. Then, in 1580, Spain acquired Ceuta when it took over the kingdom of Portugal.

In 1912, Spain took control of northern Morocco (see MOROCCO). Throughout the Rif War (1921–1926), Spain sent troops to overcome hostile Berber groups. Despite fierce resistance from the Berbers, Morocco did not gain independence again until 1956. However, Ceuta and Melilla remained Spanish territories. Today they are still governed by Spain, although Morocco would like to take them over.

Ceuta's economy depends on the ferry service with Spain. Both Ceuta and Melilla are centers for duty-free trade and some smuggling of duty-free goods across the Moroccan border. Spanish military bases occupy much of both territories and provide them with considerable income. Melilla's chief export is iron ore, mined in Morocco's Er Rif Mountains.

CLIMATE

Ceuta and Melilla experience mild winters and warm summers.

	Ceuta	Melilla
Average January temperature:	53°F (12°C)	54°F (12°C)
Average July temperature:	72°F (22°C)	76°F (24°C)
Average annual precipitation:	36 in. (91 cm)	15 in. (38 cm)

Ethnic Spanish make up about 70 percent of both populations. They are mostly Roman Catholic. Our Lady of Africa is Ceuta's patron saint. A wooden statue of her dates back to the days of Portuguese rule, when it was said to have miraculously washed up on shore. In Melilla the Church of La Conception houses a shrine dedicated to Melilla's patron saint, Our Lady, the Virgin of Victory.

Food comes from both Morocco and Spain, and both styles of cooking are to be found. Spanish meals are the most common, especially dishes of rice and locally caught seafood.

The way of life of the Spanish population is very much like that of southern Spain, with a long break from work, or siesta, being taken in the afternoon. As in many towns in mainland Spain, families and friends in Ceuta and Melilla like to promenade in the evening sunshine.

Arabic is widely spoken alongside Spanish, and about 30 percent of the population is Muslim. The Muslim population includes some Arabs and many Berbers, close relatives of those who farm in Morocco's Er Rif Mountains (see MOROCCO). Tensions have arisen between the Spanish and Islamic communities. Many Arabs and Berbers are unemployed. They are also treated less favorably in society than the Spanish majority, who fear being outnumbered by peoples who want Moroccan rule.

> **FACTS AND FIGURES**
>
> **Status:** *Autonomous community of Spain*
>
> **Area:** *13 square miles (34 square kilometers)*
>
> **Population:** *120,000*
>
> **Population density:** *9,231 per square mile (3,529 per square kilometer)*
>
> **Peoples:** *70 percent Spanish; 30 percent Berber and Arab*
>
> **Official language:** *Spanish*
>
> **Currency:** *Spanish peseta*
>
> **National day:** *Spanish National Day (October 12)*
>
> **Country's name:** *The word Ceuta is derived from the Latin word septem, meaning "seven." Seven hills make up the headland on which the town is built. Melilla may be derived from Milila or Melosa, meaning "the port of honey." Beeswax was an important export.*

Ceuta was the first European colonial territory in Africa, and today it remains one of the last.

Time line:	Ceuta and Melilla part of Roman Empire	Portugal seizes Ceuta from Arabs	Spain seizes Melilla	Ceuta becomes Spanish	Rif War	Moroccan independence. Ceuta and Melilla remain Spanish
	44 C.E.	1415	1497	1580	1921–1926	1956

Peoples of Africa

CHAD

CHAD LIES WITHIN THE SAHEL, A BELT OF DRY, DUSTY SAVANNA THAT BORDERS THE SOUTHERN SAHARA DESERT. Its western borders line the shores of Lake Chad.

Chad is the fifth largest country in Africa, a vast expanse of remote, sparsely populated wilderness. Its northern borders include the Tibesti Mountains and the trackless, sandy wastes of the Sahara. The center of the country is a land of thin, dusty grasslands, which have suffered repeated droughts over the last thirty years. The southern savanna is moister and is crossed by the Chari River. The river forms a marshy delta where it flows into Lake Chad.

An oasis at Largeau provides a resting place for travelers before they head farther north into the Sahara Desert and Tibesti Mountains. Water is a precious resource throughout the country.

90

Beyond the Desert

The lands of the Sahel (sah-HEL), the dry, dusty savanna that borders the southern Sahara, were not always as dusty and dry as they are today. About twelve thousand years ago, even the Sahara was moist and lush, the home of hippopotamuses and elephants. Early peoples left behind rock paintings in the far north of Chad in the Tibesti Mountains. The first paintings show hunters with dogs, but later examples show herders of cattle, sheep, and goats. Over thousands of years the climate changed, and overgrazing probably caused the lands to dry out.

To the west a large area of shallow water began to recede, leaving only Lake Chad. The surrounding lands served as pastures for cattle as early as 500 B.C.E. In southern Chad archaeologists have found pottery figures and funeral urns dating from about two thousand years ago. They have named this civilization the Sao (SOW) culture.

A number of large states developed in Chad from about 800 C.E. onward. The largest of these was Kanem, centered around Lake Chad. In medieval times it became part of the larger empire of Kanem-Bornu, which extended westward into what is now Nigeria. Kanem-Bornu lay on the crossroads of North African trading routes, which crossed the Sahara north to south and linked western Africa with Egypt and the Red Sea. Merchants dealt in slaves, gold, ivory, pottery, copper, and cotton.

The faith of Islam reached Chad about 1000 C.E. New Islamic sultanates emerged in the 1500s and 1600s. The most powerful were Baguirmi (buh-GEER-mee) and Wadai (wuh-DIE). Their slave traders raided the southern tribes. From 1878 onward Baguirmi, Wadai, and Kanem-Bornu came

---

FACTS AND FIGURES

Official name: République du Tchad

Status: Independent state

Capital: N'Djamena

Major towns: Sarh, Moundou, Abéché

Area: 495,625 square miles (1,284,000 square kilometers)

Population: 7,700,000

Population density: 16 per square mile (6 per square kilometer)

Peoples: Over 200 ethnic groups speaking more than 100 languages

Official languages: Arabic and French

Currency: CFA franc

National day: Independence Day (August 11)

Country's name: The country is named after Lake Chad on the western border. The origin of Lake Chad's name is unknown.

CLIMATE

Chad has a tropical climate, with most rain falling in the south between June and October. The far north is hot desert, which is gradually spreading southward into the dry grasslands of the central regions. A fierce dry wind, the harmattan, blows in from the desert during the winter.

Average January temperature: 75°F (24°C)
Average July temperature: 82°F (28°C)
Average annual precipitation: 30 in. (76 cm)

Time line:	Rock paintings in Tibesti Mountains	Cattle raising in western Chad	Sao people make pottery	States of Kanem and Bornu flourish	Kingdoms of Baguirmi and Wadai founded
	ca. 10,000 B.C.E.	ca. 500 B.C.E.	ca. 1 C.E.	ca. 800s–1700s	1500s–1600s

A Muslim festival in N'Djamena commemorates Chad gaining independence from France in 1960. People carry antique swords, flags, and ceremonial parasols.

under the domination of Rabah Zobayr, a slave trader from Sudan.

The French Colony

By the late nineteenth century, Europeans had entered the region. During the 1890s the French arrived in Chad. At that time the French were engaged in a race with other European powers to take over as much of Africa as they could. To control Chad meant that they ruled a vast region that stretched unbroken from the Mediterranean Sea to central Africa. The French allied themselves with the subjugated rulers of Baguirmi and Kanem-Bornu against Rabah Zobayr, defeating him in 1900.

French influence in the region had been confirmed by a treaty in 1897 between the two major powers of the day, Great Britain and France. Over the following thirty years, French troops fought against determined resistance, failing to defeat the Kingdom of Wadai until 1911 and the Saharan provinces of the far north until 1930.

Under French rule the people of Chad were neglected and exploited. People were uprooted from their villages to work on plantations; thousands were sent south to build railroads in Middle Congo (see CONGO, REPUBLIC OF). Cotton, the sole cash crop, was planted from 1929 on in the south of the colony. The north was a largely ignored battle zone, the scene of skirmishes and battles between the French Foreign

Chad becomes a French protectorate	French military conquest	Chad joined with French Equatorial Africa	Independence; Southerners under François Tombalbaye gain power	Rebel factions unite as Frolinat movement; civil war begins
1897	1900–1930	1910	1960	1966

Legion and local peoples who refused to recognize French authority.

During World War II (1939–1945), Chad was a base for French forces fighting German troops in the Sahara. In 1947 the independence movement in Chad was founded. Its slogan was "No more cotton, no more chiefs, no more taxes."

War and Drought

As political agitation spread through France's African colonies, the French were forced to hand over some power to the indigenous peoples. Self-government for Chad came in 1958, and full independence came two years later, although the far north remained under the control of French troops until 1965. The first president was a southerner, François Tombalbaye. The new government ran into difficulties immediately. Tombalbaye ruled as a dictator, and he soon made enemies in both the north and south. Northerners and southerners united to form a rebel movement called the National Liberation Front (Frolinat) in 1966. A disastrous and bitter thirty-year civil war followed, with France backing Tombalbaye in order to protect its economic interests in the south and Libya, Chad's neighbor, backing the rebels. In 1973, Libya exploited the chaos in Chad to seize the northern Aozou Strip and held the region until 1994.

In 1990 Idriss Dèby of the Patriotic Salvation Movement seized power. Political parties were legalized in 1992, and a nationwide cease-fire went into effect in 1996. A new democratic constitution was set up, and peace was made with Libya. Dèby was elected president, and in 1997 multiparty elections were finally held. Dèby's Patriotic Salvation Movement won a majority of seats.

As if the people of Chad hadn't suffered enough, the years 1972 and 1973 and 1979 through 1983 brought a series of devastating droughts. Starving people gathered in camps as the dust blew in from the desert. The bones of their cattle littered the sand. A deadly hazard lay in the north of the country, where large tracts of land were strewn with land mines left over from the fighting.

During the droughts of the 1970s and 80s, many people were forced to seek help in emergency camps. These women are building a makeshift shelter from sticks and hides.

1973	1990	1996	1997
Libya occupies Chad's northern territory, the Aozou Strip	Patriotic Salvation Movement led by Idriss Dèby seizes power	Nationwide ceasefire; new democratic constitution; peace made with Libya	Multiparty parliamentary elections won by Patriotic Salvation Movement

Hopes and Fears

Chad has made some recovery in recent years, but it still has to face the future as one of Africa's poorest countries. Its roads are in poor condition, and the nearest railroads are in Cameroon and Nigeria. Chad is landlocked, a long and hazardous journey away from the coast and the nearest seaports.

Cotton and livestock are the only important exports, and a few factories produce textiles and processed foods. Natron (sodium carbonate) salts around Lake Chad are a valuable resource. Other mineral deposits could help Chad considerably in years to come, including untapped reserves of uranium in the Aozou Strip near Libya. Large oil fields in the south have also been discovered.

Nearly all the people of Chad are poor. Disease is common, and doctors are few and far between. Most women undergo the surgical procedure called female genital cutting (see SOMALIA). Life expectancy is estimated at forty-six for men and forty-nine for women. Most elementary schooling is based on French models, although there are Koranic schools (based on Islamic teachings) in the north. There is some secondary schooling and a university in N'Djamena (ehn-jah-MAE-nah). Only about 40 percent of the population can read and write. Countries that send financial aid to Chad have made improving education a priority.

Chad's Peoples: How They Live

Governing the country is difficult because there are over two hundred different ethnic groups, with differences in language, dialect, religion, and customs. The country's borders, drawn up in French colonial times, bear little relation to the lands occupied by these groups. The hostility between north and south dates back to the slave trade, when northern traders raided the south for slaves, and it is reinforced by religious differences.

Over one hundred different languages and dialects may be heard in Chad. Arabic is widely spoken in the north of the

At a Koranic school in the north of the country, girls chant from Islam's holy scriptures. This region of the Sahel has been strongly Muslim for about nine hundred years.

country. Important local languages include Sara in the south and Turku in the north.

The largest group in all of Chad are the Sara (SAHR). These southern people are also the most powerful group in Chad because they have long dominated the government and army. The Sara also live across the border in the Central African Republic (see CENTRAL AFRICAN REPUBLIC). Other southern peoples include the Massa (mah-sah) and the Mundang (muhn-DAHNG). The south is a stronghold of Christianity, which is followed by one-third of Chad's population. Christianity coexists with the traditional religious beliefs of Africa.

Most southerners live by farming the land. Many use the slash-and-burn method of cultivation, where fields are cleared from different parts of the savanna each season and then allowed to grow again. This method allows the soil to rest. Other southerners labor on cotton plantations and in mills.

Crops grown for family food or local markets in the south include millet, sorghum, peanuts, and beans. Millet is pounded into a flour and mixed with water to make a dough. This is boiled and sometimes served with small amounts of hot, spiced meats or vegetable sauce. Millet is also made into a beer called *bil-bil* (BIL-bil). Some southerners fish in the Chari and Logone Rivers, preserving their catch by smoking or sun drying.

Southern villages are commonly built from mud. The homes are often round and thatched with straw. Relatives live in

A village woman pounds millet into flour with a long wooden pestle. Behind her is a typical thatched-roof granary, where grain is stored after the harvest.

homes in a family compound. Villagers store their grain crops in tall huts raised off the ground to keep the grain safe from animals. Southern men wear shirts and pants, while the women wear colorful blouses and wraps.

Central and northern Chad fall within the Islamic area of influence, and Muslims make up about 44 percent of Chad's total population. The central savanna is cattle country, and large herds of bony, long-horned steers are driven to market through the streets of N'Djamena, the capital. This

Peoples of Africa

Two Buduma fishers take to the waters of Lake Chad, which in many places is only 5 feet (1.5 meters) deep. Their boat is made from tightly bound bundles of papyrus reeds.

city includes modern and French colonial period buildings as well as the rectangular mud-brick and timber buildings common across the Sahel. The city's *grand marché* (GRAN mahr-shay), or "great market," bustles with buyers and sellers from all over the country.

Many of the central savanna peoples, such as the Kreda (KRAE-dah), live seminomadic lives, moving with their herds from dry-season encampments to farm farther south during the rainy season. Fulani (foo-LAH-nee) and Kanembu (kah-NEM-boo) cattle herders live along the western borders with Niger.

The Kotoko (KOE-toe-koe), who claim descent from the ancient Sao people, fish with nets on the waters of Lake Chad. On Lake Chad's islands live the Buduma (BOO-doo-mah) and Kuri (KOO-ree), branches of the Hausa (HOW-sah) population that stretches across western Africa (see NIGER and NIGERIA).

The peoples of the sparsely populated desert regions include the Tubu (TOO-boo) and some Tuareg (TWAHR-ehg). The

Boats of Papyrus

Lake Chad is the fourth largest lake in Africa. Its shores are flooded during the rainy season, and its levels change dramatically from one year to the next. On average, in recent years, it covers an area of 6,875 square miles (17,800 square kilometers). Its waters provide rich catches of fish, and, unfortunately, harbor schistosome, a parasite that is a serious cause of disease throughout most of Africa. The lake has many floating islands made up of tangled waterweeds and roots.

Tall, flowering reeds known as papyrus fringe Lake Chad. The ancient Egyptians used papyrus to make reed boats. The Buduma people still do. Some of the boats, which are pushed through the shallow waters with long poles, are big enough to carry ten or more passengers. Each boat, or **kaday** (kah-DAE), is made up of long bundles of reeds tightly bound by twine made from the doum palm.

It was Buduma boatbuilders who taught the Norwegian explorer Thor Heyerdahl how to make reed boats before his epic voyages across the Atlantic Ocean in *Ra I* and *Ra II* from 1969 to 1970. On his second voyage, Heyerdahl successfully reached Barbados in *Ra II*, proving that long ago, reed boats could have reached the Americas from Africa.

Tuareg live mainly in countries to the northwest (see ALGERIA, MALI, and NIGER). Both the Tubu and the Tuareg are primarily nomadic tent dwellers who move with their herds of camels, goats, and sheep from one desert water hole to another. Their herds provide meat and milk, and the desert oases (small fertile areas) provide dates, fruit, and precious water.

As in other Islamic lands south of the Sahara, men and boys wear wide tunics or robes, often of white cotton, and small round hats. The Tuareg wear turbans and wrap cloth around their faces to protect against sand and dust. Their black-blue robes are made of indigo-dyed cotton, a tradition that dates from the time before artificial dyes, when indigo was one of the few natural dyes that worked well on cotton and gave it a strong color.

Festivals and special occasions may be marked by a cavalcade of horsemen wearing long robes and small, round colorful hats and wielding antique swords, rifles, and flags to the music of trumpets and drums. Their horses are elaborately decorated with red and gold tassels. Processions such as these recall the days of the medieval sultanates and the empire of Kanem-Bornu.

> ## Deserts and Droughts
>
> *Desert peoples such as the Tubu are skilled at living in desert conditions. They move from one oasis town to another and use precious water sparingly. The date palm farmers of the Saharan oases consume about one thousand times more precious water than the nomads' livestock.*
>
> *Shortage of water also causes serious problems for the people in the Sahel. Overgrazing by cattle, sheep, and goats removes roots that trap moisture in the soil. Soil may be conserved by planting trees and windbreaks (structures to protect from the wind), by erecting fences, and by covering the ground with straw. Where agricultural land borders arid zones, new breeds of hardy millet and sorghum have been developed that are resistant to drought. This is a crucial development in lands such as Chad, where famine is always a threat.*

Young women relax inside their tent. In the dry season, some savanna peoples set up camps in pasture land where their livestock can graze.

Peoples of Africa

COMOROS

THE ISLANDS OF THE COMOROS LIE AT THE NORTHERN ENTRANCE TO THE MOZAMBIQUE CHANNEL IN THE INDIAN OCEAN. They include Grande Comore (also known as Njazidja), Mohéli (Mwali), and Anjouan (Nzwani).

The archipelago of the Comoros extends about 190 miles (303 kilometers) from north to south. The islands have coastlines of sand and black lava, occasionally fringed with mangrove swamps. Volcanic in origin, the islands are surrounded by smaller islands and reefs of coral. Steep mountain slopes covered in lush, green vegetation tower inland. The highest point is the volcanic peak Karthala, on Grande Comore, which soars to 7,749 feet (2,361 meters) above sea level.

CLIMATE

The Comoros have a tropical climate. From April to October the climate is pleasant, cooled by southeasterly winds. In November the weather turns hot and humid, and northwesterly monsoon winds bring rain.

Average January temperature: *81°F (27°C)*
Average July temperature: *75°F (24°C)*
Average annual precipitation: *113 in. (287 cm)*

The Islands of the Moon

The coast of eastern Africa is fringed with islands, from Kenya's Lamu archipelago in the north, through Zanzibar, and down to the Comoros (KAH-muh-roez) and Madagascar. In ancient times the Comoros were sometimes called the Islands of the Moon. Today, three of the Comoros make up an independent state.

The great volcanic peak of Karthala on Grande Comore has been a useful landmark to seafarers crossing the Indian Ocean since ancient times. The first people to settle the islands, probably about fifteen hundred years ago, were Malays and Polynesians who sailed from Southeast Asia. They were followed at some point by peoples from the African mainland (the ancestors of the modern Swahili) and from Madagascar. Little is known of the history of this early period because it was never written down.

Between the 900s and 1400s C.E., traders from Arabia, the Red Sea, and the Persian Gulf sailed down the coast of eastern Africa. They included Muslims called Shirazis (shi-RAH-zees), who were fleeing their homeland over a religious dispute.

COMOROS

FACTS AND FIGURES

Official name: République Fédérale Islamique des Comores

Status: Independent state

Capital: Moroni

Other towns: Mutsamudu, Fomboni, Mitsamiouli

Area: 718 square miles (1,860 square kilometers)

Population: 650,000

Population density: 905 per square mile (349 per square kilometer)

Peoples: Mixed Malagasy, African, Arab, Malay descent, French

Official languages: Arabic, French

Currency: Comorian franc

National day: Independence Day (July 6)

Country's name: Comoros comes from Djazaïr al Qamar, which means "Islands of the Moon" in the Arabic language.

the southernmost of the Comoros (see MAYOTTE). Forty-five years later, the French took advantage of the competition between the rival sultans to acquire all the islands. From 1912 onward the Comoros were governed as part of Madagascar, which was also ruled by France at that time. In 1947 the Comoros became an overseas territory of France independently of Madagascar.

A Troubled Modern State

By 1968 more and more Comorians were calling for independence, and a referendum was held on the issue in 1974. Ninety-four percent of the population voted for independence, but Mayotte went against the voting pattern, with 64 percent voting against independence (see MAYOTTE). The following year the Comoros declared their independence. France was forced to

Large ships cannot approach the port of Moroni, the capital of the Comoros on Grande Comore, because of dangerous coral reefs. Locally built wooden ships ferry the cargo ashore.

The Shirazis took over the Comoros and ruled each island as a separate and competing sultanate (Islamic kingdom). The sultans traded in spices and African slaves and used the islands' existing population as a labor force.

The Portuguese were the first Europeans to reach the Indian Ocean by sailing around Africa, and by 1527 the Comoros were appearing on European maps. The French negotiated a treaty in 1841 that gave them control of Mayotte (or Mahoré),

Time line:	Peoples of Southeast Asia, Madagascar, and the African mainland settle Comoros	Traders from Arabia, Persian Gulf and Red Sea area arrive	Islands ruled by rival sultanates	French control all the Comoros	Comoros declared an overseas territory of France
	ca. 500 C.E.	900s–1400s	900s–1800s	1886	1947

recognize this state of affairs but retained Mayotte as a French territory.

A stormy period of Comorian politics lay ahead. The first president, Ahmed Abdallah, was overthrown almost immediately by Ali Soilih, who aimed to break down class divisions and privileges and bring power to the poor peasants. Island customs and traditions were abolished, including the wearing of the veil by Muslim women. Great social disruption and opposition came from conservative religious leaders, who saw their traditional power and dominance of everyday life disappearing.

In 1978 Soilih was overthrown in a coup led by French mercenaries, and Abdallah was returned to power. He brought in a one-party, pro-French state but was assassinated in 1989. Despite French aid and cooperation, the country's economy had become weaker. Multiparty elections were held in 1990 and again in 1996, despite repeated coup attempts by foreign mercenaries. In 1996 Mohamed Taki Abdulkarim was elected president. In 1997 the island of Anjouan declared it was seceding from the Comoros. Negotiations since then have failed to persuade it to rejoin the federation.

Perfume and Poverty

The Comoros is one of the world's poorest nations. Export crops include copra (dried coconut), cloves, and vanilla pods, used in flavoring candies and desserts. The islands

The ylang-ylang, or perfume tree, has greenish yellow flowers. These are harvested in May or June to make a fragrant oil for the perfume industry.

Comoros declare independence under Ahmed Abdallah; Ali Soilih overthrows Abdallah	French-led mercenaries restore Abdallah to power; Comoros become a one-party state	Multiparty elections bring Mohamed Taki Abdulkarim to power	Anjouan secedes from Comoros
1975	**1978**	**1996**	**1997**

Fresh garden produce and big baskets lie piled up on the ground at a Comoros street market. Riyali gapvi? means "How much is that?" in the Comorian language Shimasiwa.

are most famous for the essential oils extracted from plants for the perfume industry. These include ylang-ylang (a fragrant tree), citronella, lemon grass, patchouli, and jasmine. However, the market for exotic spices and perfumes has brought scant reward in recent years. Other export crops, including sugarcane and sisal (a fibrous plant used to make twine), have been largely discontinued because they do not yield a great enough profit. Fuel and many foods must be imported.

The islands have neither industry nor mineral resources and must depend on foreign aid, much of it from France. Tourism is one industry that is not yet firmly established, but it will surely grow in the future.

Economic forces have driven many Comorians overseas. About 100,000 are thought to be working in Kenya, Tanzania, Madagascar, on the island of Réunion, and in France. The Comoros lie in an active volcanic zone, causing another domestic problem; eruptions in 1977 left some 20,000 people homeless.

Land on the Comoros is 60 percent foreign owned. Most of the rest belongs to the traditional ruling families. There is a desperate shortage of farmland, and clearing of natural vegetation has led to precious soil being washed away. Eighty-five percent of the population grow some food for their own needs. Comorian dishes make use of rice (which is mostly imported), cassava (a starchy root crop), corn, sweet potatoes, coconuts, and bananas. Curries and samosas (pastry envelopes of meat or vegetables) are popular. Common local spices include cardamom seeds, coriander, nutmeg, and cinnamon. The cooking has Asian, African, and French influences. Coconut milk is drank mixed with fresh fruit juice.

Peoples of Africa

A group of Comorian women sing and dance, beating the time with wooden sticks and clappers. They are dressed in colorful cotton wraps typical of the region.

The Comorian Way of Life

The various immigrants who settled the Comoros over the ages—Malay, Polynesian, Arab, Persian, Madagascan, mainland African—have intermingled to form a largely mixed society in which there is little ethnic strife. Arabic and French are official languages, but the most widely spoken language is Shimasiwa (shi-mah-SEE-wah).

Culturally, the Comoros are most closely linked with the other islands of eastern Africa's Swahili-speaking coast. These lay

Let's Talk *Shimasiwa*

Shimasiwa is made up of the easternmost dialects of Swahili, the language that originated along the east African coast and on its islands. In structure, Swahili is a Bantu language that includes Arabic, Persian, Hindi, Portuguese, and English words. Shimasiwa shows the influence of French pronunciation. The dialect varies from one island to another.

salama (sah-LAH-muh)	hello
bariza soubouni (buh-REE-zuh soo-BOO-nee)	good morning
karibu (kah-REE-boo)	welcome
habare sa? (hah-BAH-rae sah)	how are you?
lala ha unono (lah-lah HAH oo-NOE-noe)	goodnight
tafatvali (tah-fah-TWAH-lee)	please
marahaba (mah-rah-HAH-bah)	thank you

Fishing, too, is a valuable source of food. Local catches include shark, tuna, scad, and grouper. Marine turtles, which breed locally, were once a Comorian delicacy. They have been hunted to the brink of extinction but are now being protected.

Malaria and other diseases are common, but health care is minimal. For men, life expectancy is estimated to be fifty-six and for women, fifty-seven. Schools offer a basic education for children ages seven to sixteen, and about six out of ten adults can read and write.

Weddings and Music

Weddings are among the most important events in the social life of the islands, marked by dancing and feasting over several days. Drumming and dance play an important part in everyday life. The music is mostly that of the lively Swahili tradition known as taarab *(tah-RAHB), which combines traditional and modern African, Arabian, and Indian styles with poetic songs. Taarab (from the Arabic word* tariba, *meaning "to be moved") is popular all along the east African coast, even as far away as Somalia and the Persian Gulf.*

A wedding is celebrated on the island of Mohéli. The groom wears green. The women sit separately from the men. White make-up is an island tradition.

on the ancient trading routes favored by the wooden ships called dhows. The triangular sails of dhows are still a familiar sight in Indian Ocean waters. Smaller dhows sail between the islands today.

The traditional building material on the Comoros is a cement made from crushed coral, although modern building materials are now also widely used. In Moroni and Mutsamudu there are whitewashed walls, courtyards, mazes of narrow streets and alleys, mosques, and busy street markets. Rainwater from the monsoon season is collected and stored in tanks.

A few Comorians are Roman Catholic Christians, but most are Muslims. Islamic tradition holds Comorian society together, and the festivals of the Muslim calendar are the chief celebrations of the year. Most important of all is Eid al-Fitr, which marks the end of Ramadan, a month of fasting. Comorians may travel to Islamic festivals as far away as the island of Lamu, off northern Kenya, more than 700 miles away.

Comorians still ply their traditional crafts, including metalwork, pottery, basketry, and intricate wood carving, used in making doors, chests, and furniture. Muslim women wrap themselves in black veils. In accordance with Islamic practice, the veils are pulled across the face when women are away from home. Women of African origin wear the boldly patterned *kitenge* (kee-TEHN-gae) cloth popular along the east African coast. Traditionally, men dress in white and wear embroidered skullcaps called *coffias* (koh-FEE-ahs).

Glossary

AIDS: *a*cquired *i*mmuno*d*eficiency *s*yndrome, a normally fatal disease often passed on by sexual intercourse. It is caused by the virus HIV (*h*uman *i*mmunodeficiency *v*irus), which attacks the body's ability to resist disease and infection.

ancestor worship: the worship of deceased people from whom a community or family are descended.

archaeology: the scientific study of things and places of past human life and activities.

archipelago: a large group of islands.

aristocratic: belonging to the nobility, an elite or privileged group within society.

cavalcade: a procession of people on horseback.

CFA franc: franc de la Communauté Financière Africaine (franc of the African Financial Community). This is a unit of currency shared by various African countries that were formerly French colonies.

coup: a change of government brought about by force.

democratic: conforming with the principles of rule by the people, in which government is carried out by representatives elected by the public.

desalination: removing salt from seawater so that it can be used for drinking or for irrigation of crops.

duty-free: able to be purchased without payment of the usual taxes.

equatorial: relating to regions close to the equator, an imaginary line drawn on maps around the middle of the world. A typical equatorial climate is hot and wet all year-round.

French Equatorial Africa: a former federation of French territories in central Africa, made up at various times between 1908 and 1958 of Ubangi-Shari (now Central African Republic), Chad, Middle Congo (now the Republic of Congo), and Gabon.

highlife: a Westernized form of African music and dance that developed during colonial rule. It is popular in western Africa.

incorruptible: a person who is honest and who will not change his or her mind if offered money to do so.

jihad: a holy war fought by Muslims. Muslims consider it a religious duty.

Koranic schools: classrooms attached to mosques (buildings where Muslim people pray). Boys go there to learn how to read Arabic and to study the faith of Islam.

landlocked: having no access to the ocean; surrounded by other countries.

language groups: separate, but related, languages spoken by different peoples who long ago spoke the same language.

literacy rate: the percentage of people who can read and write.

malnutrition: suffering or ill health caused by a poor diet or insufficient food.

millet: a hardy cereal crop grown for food, drink, and fodder.

pestle: a rod or pole used for grinding materials in a bowl or container called a mortar.

pidgin: a simplified form of speech that is a mix of two or more languages. Pidgin languages are used for communication between groups that do not speak the same language.

republic: a country in which power rests with the people and their elected representatives. A president usually heads a republic.

savanna: a grassland dotted with trees and drought-resistant undergrowth.

separatist: someone who wants part of one country to break away from the rest and become a separate state.

sorghum: various types of cereal crop, some of which are used for food and fodder.

staging post: a stopping point on a route, such as a place for refueling or loading food.

subsistence farming: growing crops for one's own use rather than selling them.

sultanate: the territory ruled by a sultan; an Islamic kingdom.

Further Reading

Internet Sites
Look under Countries A to Z in the Atlapedia Online Web Site at
    http://www.atlapedia.com/online/countries
Look under country listing in the CIA World Factbook Web Site at
    http://www.odci.gov/cia/publications/factbook
Look under country listing in the Library of Congress Country Studies Web Site at
    http://lcweb2.loc.gov/frd/cs/cshome.html

Burkina Faso
Koslow, Philip. *Hausaland: The Fortress Kingdoms*. Broomall, PA: Chelsea House, 1995.
Mack-Williams, Kibibi. *Mossi*. New York: Rosen Group, 1996.
Ndukwe, Pat I. *Fulani*. New York: Rosen Group, 1995.

Burundi
Twagilimana, Aimable. *Hutu and Tutsi*. New York: Rosen Group, 1997.
Wolbers, Marian F. *Burundi*. Broomall, PA: Chelsea House, 1989.

Cameroon
Aniakor, Chike C. *Fang*. New York: Rosen Group, 1996.
Burnham, Philip. *Gbaya*. New York: Rosen Group, 1996.
Hathaway, Jim. *Cameroon in Pictures*. Minneapolis, MN: Lerner Publishing Group, 1989.

Canary Islands
See web sites mentioned above on Spain

Cape Verde
See web sites mentioned above

Central African Republic
See web sites mentioned above

Ceuta and Melilla
See web sites mentioned above on Spain

Chad
Baroin, Catherine. *Tubu: The Teda and the Daza*. New York: Rosen Group, 1997.
Greenblatt, Miriam. *Chad*. Danbury, CT: Children's Press, 1998.

Comoros
See web sites mentioned above

Index

Abdallah, Ahmed, 100
Abdulkarim, Mohamed Taki, 100
Adama, Modibo, 67
Adamawa, Emirate of, 67
Ahidjo, Alhaji Ahmadou, 68
Aka, 86
Anzica, 83
Aozou Strip, Chad, 93, 94
Arabic: in the Central African Republic, 87; in Ceuta and Melilla, 89; in Chad, 94–95; in the Comoros, 102
Arabs in Ceuta and Melilla, 88, 89
Arts and crafts: in Burkina Faso, 54; in Cameroon, 74–75, *74*
Azande, 83

Babinga, 86, *86*
Baguirmi, 91–92
Baka, *65*, 73–74
Bakouma, Central African Republic, 85
Balundu, *68*
Bamileke, 68, 71, 74–75
Bamoun, 74
Banda, 83, 86
Bangassou, Central African Republic, *82*
Bangui, Central African Republic, 85, 86
Bantu-speakers, 65–66
Banziri, 86–87
Baya, 83, 86
Belgians in Burundi, 59–60
Berbers, 88, 89
Berimbau, 80
Bil-bil, 95
Biya, Paul, 68
Bobo, 54, *54*
Boganda, Barthélemy, 84
Bokassa, Jean-Bédel, 84, *84*, 86
Bomu River, Central African Republic, *82*
Bouar, Central African Republic, 83
British people in Cameroon, 66, 67
Buduma, 96, *96*
Buhake, 59
Bujumbura, Burundi, 63
Burkinabe, 53
Busani, 54
Buyoya, Pierre, 60–61

Cachupa, 81
Catholics: in Burkina Faso, 54; in Burundi, 62; in the Canary Islands, 77; in Cape Verde, 80; in the Central African Republic, 85; in Ceuta and Melilla, 89; in the Comoros, 103
Chad, Lake, 96, *96*
Chari River, Chad, 95
Christians: in Cameroon, 69; in Chad, 95. *See also* Catholics, Protestants

Cimboa, 80
Climate change: in Burkina Faso, 56; in Chad, 91
Clothing: in Chad, 97; in the Comoros, 103
Coffias, 103
Coladeira, 80
Compaore, Blaise, 53
Crioulu, 80

Dacko, David, 84
Dance: in Burundi, 61; in Cameroon, 75, *75*; in the Comoros, 103
Dèby, Idriss, 93
Dhows, 103
Dibango, Manu, 74
Douala, Cameroon, 70, 71
Douala language, 69
Drummers of Burundi, 61
Dutch people in Cameroon, 66
Dyula language, 54
Dyula people, 54

Education: in Burkina Faso, 56; in Burundi, 63, *63*; in Cameroon, 70, 72; in Cape Verde, 81; in the Central African Republic, 85, *85*; in Chad, 94, *94*; in the Comoros, 102
Eid al-Fitr, 103
English language in Cameroon, 69
Evora, Cesaria, 80

Fang, 71, 75
Farming: in Burkina Faso, 55–56; in Burundi, *59*, 62; in Cameroon, 69, *69*, 71, *71*; in the Canary Islands, 77, *77*; in Cape Verde, 80; in the Central African Republic, 85; in Chad, 95; in the Comoros, 101
FESPACO, 57
Fishing: in Burundi, 62; in the Canary Islands, 77; in Cape Verde, 80; in Chad, 96; in the Comoros, 102
Food: in Burkina Faso, 55–56, *55*; in the Canary Islands, 77; in Cape Verde, 81, *81*; in the Central African Republic, 87; in Ceuta and Melilla, 89; in Chad, 95; in the Comoros, 101, *101*
Franco, Francisco, 77
French Equatorial Africa, 83
French language: in Burkina Faso, 54; in Burundi, 62; in Cameroon, 69; in the Central African Republic, 87; in the Comoros, 102
French people: in Burkina Faso, 52–53; in Cameroon, 66, 67; in the Central African Republic, 83–84; in Chad, 92–93; in the Comoros, 99–100
French West Africa, 52–53

Fulani language, 69
Fulani people, 54, 66–67, 71–72, 96

Ganwa, 59
Gaoga, 83
Germans: in Burundi, 59; in Cameroon, 67
Gitega, Burundi, 59
Gombo, 87
Grunshi, 54
Guanches, 76

Hausa language, 69, 87
Hausa people, 54, 96
Health care: in Burkina Faso, 56–57; in Cameroon, 70, *70*; in Cape Verde, 81; in the Central African Republic, 85; in Chad, 94; in the Comoros, 102
Heyerdahl, Thor, 96
Housing: in Burundi, *62*, 63; in Cameroon, 73, *73*, 74; in Cape Verde, *79*, 80–81; in the Central African Republic, 86, 87; in Chad, 95, 96; in the Comoros, 103
Hutu, 58–59, 60–62, *60*, 63

Industry: in Burkina Faso, 56; in Cameroon, 69; in the Canary Islands, 77; in Chad, 94
Inuzu, 63

Kaday, 96
Kamerun, 67
Kanem, 91
Kanem-Bornu, 91–92
Kanembu, 96
Kapsigi, 72
Kirdi, 71–73
Kirundi, 62
Kitenge, 103
Kola, 73–74
Kolingba, André, 84
Korup National Park, Cameroon, 72
Kotoko, 96
Kreda, 96
Kuri, 96

Languages: in Burkina Faso, 54; in Burundi, 62; in Cameroon, 68–69; in Cape Verde, 80; in the Central African Republic, 87; in Ceuta and Melilla, 89; in Chad, 94–95; in the Comoros, 102
Lanzarote, Canary Islands, 77
Largeau, Chad, *90*
Lobi, 54
Logone River, Chad, 95
Louis Rwagasore, Prince, 60

Makosso, 74

Page numbers in *italic* indicate illustrations.

Malays in the Comoros, 98
Mambila, 74
Mande-speakers, 54
Mandja, 86
Margi, 72
Massa, 95
Mbaïki, 86
Mindelo, Cape Verde, *79*
More, 54
Morna, 80
Moroni, Comoros, *99*, 103
Mossi, 51–53, *52*, 54, 55
Mundang, 95
Music: in Burundi, 61, *61*; in Cameroon, 74, 75; in Cape Verde, 80; in the Comoros, 103
Muslims: in Burkina Faso, 54, *57*; in Burundi, 62; in Cameroon, 67, *67*, 70, 71–72; in the Central African Republic, 85; in Ceuta and Melilla, 88, 89; in Chad, 91, *92*, *94*, 95; in the Comoros, 98–99, 103
Mutsamudu, Comoros, 103
Mwami, 59

Ndadaye, Melchior, 61
N'Djamena, Chad, 94, 95–96
Nyos, Lake; Cameroon, 73

Ouagadougou, Burkina Faso, *52*, 57, *57*
Ouedreaogo, Idrissa, 57

Patassé, Ange-Félix, 84
Phoenicians in Ceuta and Melilla, 88
Pidgin English in Cameroon, 69

Polynesians in the Comoros, 98
Portuguese language in Cape Verde, 80
Portuguese people: in Cameroon, 66; in Cape Verde, 78
Protestants: in Burundi, 62; in Cape Verde, 80; in the Central African Republic, 85

Religions: in Burkina Faso, *52*, 54–55, *57*; in Burundi, 62; in Cameroon, 69–70, 71–72, 73, 74; in the Canary Islands, 77; in Cape Verde, 80; in the Central African Republic, 85; in Ceuta and Melilla, 88, 89; in Chad, 91, *92*, *94*, 95; in the Comoros, 103
Romans in Ceuta and Melilla, 88
Ruanda-Urundi, 59–60
Rwagasore, Prince Louis, 60

Salsa mojo, 77
Samo, 54
Sango, 87
Sankara, Thomas, 53
Sao culture, 91
Sara language, 95
Sara people, 86, 95
Senufo, 54
Shimasiwa, 102
Shirazis, 98–99
Slave trade: in Cameroon, 66, *66*, 67; in Cape Verde, 78; in the Central African Republic, 83; in Chad, 91–92, 94; in the Comoros, 99
Soccer, 75
Soilih, Ali, 100

Spanish language in Ceuta and Melilla, 89
Spanish people: in the Canary Islands, 76; in Ceuta and Melilla, 88, 89
Sports and games: in Cameroon, 75; in the Canary Islands, 77
Swahili, 62, 87

Taarab, 103
Tombalbaye, François, 93
Tourism: in the Canary Islands, 77; in the Comoros, 101
Tuareg, 96–97
Tubu, 96–97
Turku, 95
Tutsi, 58–59, *59*, 60–62, 63, *63*
Twa, 58, 59, 62, 63

Ubangi River, Central African Republic, 87
Ubangi-Shari, 83
Upper Volta, 52–53

Voltaic language-speakers, 54

Wadai, 91–92

Yakoma, 86–87
Yaméogo, Maurice, 53
Yaoundé, Cameroon, 70

Zande, 86
Zobayr, Rabah, 92

Page numbers in *italic* indicate illustrations.